Dear Anonymous

Stories told by you

Prose by

Sara Sheehan

Dear Anonymous

Stories are in no order

Feel free to start wherever you'd like.

Dear Anonymous

Instagram @moonsoulchild

Twitter @moonssoulchild

Facebook @moonsoulchild

Also, follow **@dearanonymousbook** on Instagram!

Dear Anonymous,

I chose to put together this collection for you. I wanted to give more. I know you're asking yourself "Dear Anonymous" "What could this be", let me explain, this collection is stories told by you, on topics including: love, self-love, self-acceptance, mental health, toxicity, friendships, relationships, anything along these lines. This collection is to hear your story because I know how hard it is to be heard and understood. In these pieces you don't need to fear because you will be ANONYMOUS, you may tell your story in the realest version, whether you are currently going through it, or past tense, please tell your whole story. After your story, there may be a response from me as I reflect on your story and find a piece of myself in there. Some stories may be without a response, because I cannot attach myself to everyone story, I have not felt or was a part of. For the stories I don't have a responses for, there will be blank pages for anyone reading to reflect, because I know there are some out there reading saying "I felt that" "How did you know" and might want to share their story if they didn't get the chance, this is your chance. This collection is filled with pain, a ton of heart break and burdens carried that are being let go of and trying desperately to heal from. I told my story in my previous books "The Journey Through My Heart 1&2" "I Was Never Broken" and "Letters to You" but you will find pieces of my

story along these pieces as well. There will also be
pieces of my poetry and prose spread out the book
from experts of my favorite pieces from other books
of mine, and some new, that tie into related topics
of this collection. I pray whoever reads this, will
one day open and tell their story without fear
because being true to yourself and the pain will
only bring you closure towards those burdens. I pray
whoever reads can't intentionally relate, because
relating to any of this pain is not what I would
wish upon anyone. If you can relate, or have once
upon a time, I pray you are in a better place now,
and these words are encouragement to never let
yourself fall into those habits of bad behavior. I
pray whoever reads this will understand we are all
human and we all felt pain, even if it is not the
same exact feeling, we have all felt some piece of
what it feels like to be damaged, heart-broken,
lost, not good enough, worthless, the list goes on.
I pray you see these things were temporary
roadblocks, and you needed to rise above them to
become the strongest version, to open and love you.

Anonymous 1

I started to struggle with food just after I
turned 8, ever since I've been stuck in a cycle of
being okay, restricting, starving, and purging.
It's something I've realized will always be a part
of my life. I'm still working on coming to terms
with that, and I'm not fully sure how to do that.
I self-harmed for the first time at 11. I'm now 17,
and it's basically consumed my entire teenage life.
I wish I could go back and stop myself that very
first time, but I can't. It's a weird one because

I rely on it, but I hate it and myself for doing it. I've gone months without it and then months without going a day not doing it. It's terrifying because the longer it goes on, and the worse it gets, the more encouragement you give yourself to keep doing it and to keep going that little bit further. It's like, you're okay after that, so you can do it worse next time. It's the first thing I think of in situations, when I'm struggling or unhappy, when I've made a mistake, even when I'm happy. I can't truly express how I feel about it other than I hate it with my entire being, but I need it to keep going. My reasons for it are even blurred now, is it for the pain? The blood? Do I just think I deserve it? I genuinely don't know anymore, and I can't remember what it's like to not see cuts and scars when I see myself, I don't even know how people go from the secrecy of self-harm, to the complete opposite in recovery.

I also struggle with anxiety, and panic attacks are something I had to learn to adapt to. I don't fully understand my triggers or even how to handle them, and I've had them for over 5 years now. I'm not sure I'll ever have those answers. I find it weird how little I care about my life, I don't understand why my mental health is the way it is, how this isn't normal for everyone but also how it's normal for me.

Dear Anonymous

Out of all the stories I read and gave my input, this story stuck out the most to me, and not because of your self-harm, but because of the way

you see it, how you normalize it, how it's become
of you, as you speak. I want to first address, you
don't deserve the self-inflicted pain you bring
upon yourself, as you state "you're not sure why
you come to this conclusion" every time, but I want
to share with you, I don't know you, I've never
lived a day in your life, or walked a day in the
darkness of your mind, but I'm here on the outside
looking in and I'm here to tell you you're life
matters, just like mine and many others. Whether I
self-harmed, or never did, it all comes back to the
way our mind takes over when the dark clouds rise
and we don't know what to do, but to inflict pain
upon ourselves. Pain meaning, physical, emotionally,
or mentally, pain is pain and we all go through
something we never feel we can come back from, so I
get the sense of feeling like there's no good that
comes from a life that feels lifeless. I learned a
lot in my 25 years of life, and that is, the most
important person in your life is yourself. I know
when it comes to choose, we would rather have people
in our corner, but if those people aren't giving us
something positive to add to our lives, we need to
leave them behind. I'm not one who takes on stress
easily, I cry, I cry a lot and sometimes I think the
scariest thoughts. I have become terrified of death
growing older has made it worse, thinking about
loved ones dying, or myself, and I work myself up
more. I can't stand working anywhere that makes me
feel less of myself. I can't be around anyone who
makes me feel I'm not worth being accepted, or I'm
only worth being used. I don't take stress of life
easily, but I have come to terms with managing it. I
cry when I need to, I write when I need a release,
and I remind myself this is the only life I have,

and every problem I face is just another roadblock, and another blessing is on its way. I struggle with anxiety, and I've been very depressed, so I can relate to those random panic attacks without reason. I can say I isolated myself from a lot of people I loved because I was just anxious, about, everything. I still have my moments, some are worse than others, and some have triggers, but I use a lot of grounding coming to terms with the anxiety upfront and acknowledge it like it's a person who hurt me, and use it as a lesson for the next time it comes to visit me. Don't let something that hurts you become a "normal feeling". Your mental health is important. I know what I say won't bring you to the solution, but I hope it brings you through it. I pray for you in this time of your life, with lots of love. I pray you can find the beauty in your life and in yourself. I pray you come to terms with letting go of the habit of hurting yourself to hide the pain, I promise there's better ways to remind yourself how important you are.

Anonymous 2

My siblings and I were abandoned by our mother a month before my high school graduation. She was in and out our lives for 2/3 years prior. I had to grow up fast. I didn't have a life during my teen years. My father taught me everything I knew, being Puerto Rican, the women are head of the household, cook, clean, I took care of everything. I went to school, worked, did a lot of house chores and helped my dad with my siblings. Prior to her leaving us, my father took us in because my mother left me and my siblings in my aunt's house (my father's sister). We were with my mother before because she gave my dad an ultimatum; her or his mom. At the time we lived in Florida and my dad wanted to fly back to New York because his mom was in the hospital, seriously ill with diabetes and her leg was amputated. A year later my grandma passed away. Seeing my dad as a single parent, raising 3 kids, he struggled. He tried the best he could to make us happy, but at times, it was bad. We moved a lot. Lived in a trailer home that had 3 rooms. The other 2 rooms were rented out to 2 grown men, while my father, siblings and I lived in another room. All shares a kitchen and bathroom. We also were homeless at a point, and at times slept in the car next to the church we attended. My heart is so heavy, I had to go through so much because of her choice. I get so emotional at times because I didn't have that mother everyone else had growing up. Having that bond, developing as a young woman by myself (because my father didn't really know how to help me or explain anything). I had my 1st period without her there to help. She didn't teach me anything a mother should teach their daughter. I had to learn from myself or from other women in the family, and my dad. It's so hard to explain the pain I have in my heart because of her. I have abandonment issues. I fear the ones I love will leave me. I have major trust issues from her because she tried coming back into my life but left again, and due to being used by men in my previous relationships. I also have bad anxiety. It just really hurts, the one who brought you into this world, gives up and leaves you. I'm happy to say, I'm currently in a loving relationship, but I do need constant reassurance and I'm terrified it will affect us sooner or later, but my boyfriend is patient and helpful with my healing process. My mother's choice made me stronger, I wouldn't have been the women I am today without the pain, I still love with every piece of me and hopefully when I have children of my own, I will never be like her.

Dear Anonymous

The love missing from a parent, is the kind that will have you questioning whether it's your worth, or your mistake, but also something you will may never understand, because even when there's an explanation, we still blame us. The scariest part is having it happen time and time again, with anyone you love going forward, when you're abandoned and you're alone with your mind. Your thoughts can be a dark place, I've thought somethings I never thought I could. I've been to that dark place, too. I didn't see my father for about 10 years, he never spoke of the reason he decided to just leave. My parents broke up, but we still spent the weekend with my dad. He took me and my sister out to dinner, for ice cream, even attended all my school field trips. He was cool, he always made the other kids in the class laugh. These memories I remember, but there's not so many I do. From my freshman year in high school, till 2017 I had no contact with him. Until he requested me on Facebook, and everything is completely different now. He's reasoning for being gone never surfaced and I'm faced without "closure" or the story behind why me and my sister grew up without him. It's like you see life in a different set of eyes, I grew up to be very wise. I

love wholeheartedly, it sometimes gets the best of
me. I' ve once abandoned a friend, chose one day to
never text her back, never heard a word from her.
Don' t blame yourself for the toxicity of someone
you love, it' s draining. No matter the
relationship, friendship, or family. If it' s toxic
to your being, alters your energy, make peace with
it, then walk away. If it comes to second chances,
don' t forget it' s always your choice, it' s your
life, your heart, you protect it. And if someone
walks out your life, don' t blame yourself. Just
remember not everyone will take the same road,
they' re not a part of your growth. It' s okay.

Anonymous 3

I was with my ex for a year, going into 2017
we became distant, not being able to spend much time
together because of our schedules. It started
getting between us. He went on a trip and had a girl
come back to his room. When he came back home, he
was planning to keep us together, but couldn' t deal
with the weight of what he did. He left our home,
admitted what he done was wrong and wanted to stay,
but felt bad for the other girl. She had money to
pay for his schooling. He swore for months he would
come back. He would always show up at my house,
work, school, crying saying not to give up because
he was only staying with her so she could help him
financially after he spent school money on the trip.
I last saw him when he showed up at my school in
October after intentionally getting a job across the
street. We are here, one and half years later, have
not spoken in a month. Last time we spoke he asked
to see me to get brunch, or to the gym, I said to

get permission from our current significant others because it is obviously unacceptable. He told his two best friends that he's stuck, he messed up, and wants to finish school so he can be where he wants, also has admitted to still missing me and regretting what he did. I moved on, but never let go. He was my first love. I feel in my heart we are still connected but have no way finding out. I cut his best friend's hair last week, and he stated, "he asked me to come here without you knowing because he is scared of how you will react".

Dear Anonymous

I'm all about giving second chances when it is due. But there comes a time where you'll have no more chances to give and you'll feel drained. Taking the same person back after the first time never feels the same, everything will feel different. And now, you have your guard all the way up, wondering if he will repeat it again. I honestly believe their heart is in the right place, but they don't know how to use it. A lot of time they want their cake and eat it too. The more you allow the more he will keep doing it. The part I really don't agree with is that she pays for his school, and he doesn't want to leave her because of that. Very selfish, material things don't matter when it comes to love and your dreams are important, but no one can help you make your dreams come true, but you. No money can make it come true. He needs to learn how to be a man and do for himself before he thinks to love other. I can't comment whether it's truly love or not because I don't feel how you feel, but I will say I have been where you are, I've been the girl who took him back many times and come to find out the whole time we dated he was cheating on me, which I didn' t find out until three years later. I was no longer angry. I was happy I got out of the situation because all it did was bring me pain. Sometimes we love the thought of love and attach it to someone because we want to be loved. It' s hard to know when love is real, and the love that' s only alive within us. I don' t believe in second chances no more when it comes to real pain, but I do believe it does take time to understand the pain you felt, which makes it hard to let go. You' ll never let the person who is meant for you find you if you keep hurting yourself, and everyone you meet because you keep running back to him. You' re hurting yourself more by sticking around than letting go. It' s the closest I could feel to how you feel. It' s true a lot of us really attach love to someone we want to love and their nowhere close to what we deserve. To think, making someone love you, and if it does, it' ll always be flawed in a way the pain will never let you see the brighter days, because every day will feel like a challenge of making the other person happy, you' re draining all the energy you have trying to make something work that will never work. Don' t waste time that can be pursued into other areas. It' s hard for the heart to let go, but we just need to be honest with them, straight up, no second chances.

Anonymous 4

I don' t know what to do, my ex is always making me insecure. He always checks out other woman right in front of me, to the point it really started

affecting me, now I feel as if I wasn' t enough.
I' m not sure how to love myself again.

Dear Anonymous

You were beautiful before him, while you were
with him, and now. He didn' t define your beauty.
Just because he checks out other women doesn' t mean
you' re not beautiful. If he did it even though you
told him it bothered you, I would say he wasn' t a
person with a heart like yours. You can' t make
someone see your beauty. Your beauty is way deeper
than what meets the public eye. Think about your
heart, how you love, and how you show everyone you
love your heart openly. That is your real beauty.
Don' t let anyone take that from you.

Anonymous 5

I had a bad mental breakdown this Saturday,
and it got me thinking about everything and everyone
in my life. Specifically, the people I was with that
day. I finally felt okay today, until my friend told
me the guy, I was talking to had messaged her and
asked if she' d like to hang out with him this
weekend. Nothing wrong with that. It' s just I
thought of him, and I had a connection, or he was
interested in me. I know this action doesn' t really
mean anything, but I' m feeling self-conscious about
it, because I' m usually not the "pretty" girl, in
these situations. I tend to not let it get to me
because I know I have good qualities and pretty in
my own way. It' s just difficult when these things
happen that make me think otherwise. I just don' t

know how to get myself to think differently and to not let it get to me. Most of all, to keep loving myself despite someone else not loving me or thinking I am beautiful enough.

Dear Anonymous

The thing is, sometimes we get caught up in how we feel and forget the other person feelings, and what they want. We create an illusion on what we want and not think twice. Then sometimes, others have a way of making you love them and leaving like you were nothing or lead you to somewhere you cannot explain the feeling, but you'll feel it. We sometimes want the things that are not reciprocated.

Anonymous 6

I just went through a breakup, I spent so much money on him, I spent 1,000 on a trip down to see him where he lives and then he broke up with me four days later! I would love to hear your words on not losing hope in love after you get dragged through the mud by someone you thought loved you.

Dear Anonymous

Losing someone is one of the hardest things no matter what the case is, it hurts. The hardest part about letting go is we love them, or at least thought we did. It's unfortunate, how the heart can continue loving people who only bring us pain. It makes no sense, but you were meant to meet everyone in your life for a reason, you can't analyze every single relationship or friendship you connect with, when it's over, you'll know. There's nothing I can tell you that will make the pain feel less, but I can tell you that you don't drown yourself in pain that no longer serves its purpose in your life. The longer you hold on to it, the longer you go without finding it again.

Anonymous 7

My cousin who was also my best friend and like sister to me, committed suicide on September 11, 2018. Since then, I've been suffering so much missing her. I feel like a part of me died with her. I also tried to write poetry to help cope with the pain. It has been getting manageable to deal with, but it's never the same. Whenever something new happens to me I miss texting her about it. I wish I could have done or said something to help her when I could, but she made her decision to leave and nothing stopped her.

Dear Anonymous

The loss of anyone you love is painful. It stings, it scars, it's always felt. The feeling of guilt clouds our mind when we feel we could have done more, said more, or could have saved them. But truly, it's not your job to save anyone, it's only in the cards for you to love them. I remember when my Poppy gave us a scare, he had to be revived, which he did, and went into the nursing home to get recovered. He overdosed on his pain medicine he took for his back, because my Nana was sick, and he

didn't want to be without her. This was January of
2009, the night after my cousin Shayla passed away,
I spoke with my Poppy on the phone and I remember he
said "I didn't see you tonight, I just wanted to
call and say hi" and that night he passed, and I
felt guilty because I chose not to see him that
night, but I didn't let it beat me up because I did
speak to him, and we exchanged words, I love you,
and that was his way of letting me know he'll
always be near. My Nana passed in March of the same
year. 3 people who were close, very close to me, all
left the same year. I didn't experience anyone
close to me who took their life, but death is all
the same when it comes to the pain we endure while
trying to heal from the loss. We blame ourselves. We
guilt trip ourselves. We drown in the pain, and
it's okay, they teach us how to swim through it,
and live with their spirit.

You will never rise from a heart break

if you soak in the pain,

instead of planting new seeds

for growth and healing.

Anonymous 8

How do I cut off worthless people if I've been treated poorly my whole life?

Dear Anonymous

Just because you've been treated badly your whole life doesn't give you reason to play victim to being treated poorly your whole life. What you allow, will always continue, remember that. The more you let them treat you bad, the more they will. Learn the lesson they presented to you and cut them off. Attaching yourself to people who only bring you pain all you will receive is pain.

Anonymous 9

I was with someone for almost three years. We lived together then he ended things two months ago, and the day I moved out he took another girl to San Fran and ended up catching an STD. He always tells me he needs to do him and figure himself out. He would always keep saying we are "on pause" and he loves me and misses me so much, and he is hurting from the breakup too. I feel he keeps playing mind games, he wants to keep me on the back burner. I need closure but a part of me wants him, but I know that be the dumbest thing ever.

Dear Anonymous

You're not dumb for loving someone with all your heart, to want someone who is no good for you. People with good hearts have the most trouble with this, we see the best in people and expect them to see the same in us. But you cannot make someone love you the same, and that's why someone who doesn't love or value you, ever will. If they can wake up one day and decide they no longer love you, let them go. Let them go the second they give you that sign. It gets hard because sometimes they're never straight up about how they feel, sometimes you're trying to find the answers, but don't believe it means there is hope. There's no need to attach these crazy ideas that love will revisit again like the first time you fell in love with them. Stop letting them come back when they please, while they left you without wonder.
You do not *deserve to wait around for a love, that'
unclear, undecided, and gone.*

Anonymous 10

I got out of an emotional abusive situationship that lasted almost two years. I blocked him on all social media and slowly getting over him. He's in my close group of friends and whenever we go out, I end up seeing him, I don't want to create a scene and be angry with him, but I can't act like everything is okay. Right now, I have a lot of hatred towards him, he said some really, awful things to me the last time we talked.

We have this constant toxic cycle going on and recently he called me asking to be friends, and during the phone call he asked if we can get together again, I told him he hurt me too much and I can't handle it. We became friends again and he continued to disrespect me. I feel like whenever I see him, I act like I'm okay, and we end up bringing up our past. Is there a point in becoming friends?

Dear Anonymous

I know you don't want to keep reliving the past every time you see him, but you will. The sad part of loving someone, is the memories are always there, no matter the situation or timing, seeing them will instantly make you remember. You feel every emotion you last felt when you left things, but that doesn't mean it's real. You let go, you left it all behind you. Don't let the past control you, convincing yourself he has control over you. When you're around each other think of all the reasons you left, and where you're at now, and compare the differences and why you decided to leave. Repeat them until you're no longer mad, upset, or sad. You'll be able to look at him, smile, and wish him the best. The pain he brought upon you is no longer holding you down from happiness, you're happier now without him and you need to remember that. Remember, there's no point in holding on to grudges that only effect you in the end. The next time you see him, look at him, and remember everything you feel intensely, but you'll also look at him and feel nothing, and that'll be a sign you finally accepted it wasn't your loss all along, it was his. You always continue the same patterns with toxic people, they swear they will change, and you always end up at questioning why you thought it was impossible, to keep trying to save them when you know you do not have the strength to keep giving your energy away, and your heart, so easily.

Anonymous 11

I had my first same sex relationship experience. My best friend, of four years, asked me to be her girlfriend. We were together one month when she came out to her mom. From there she was outed, embarrassed, mistreated, and rejected by her family. They claim they're not homophobic, but that I betrayed the family by becoming more than friends, so I wasn't allowed to be near the family. We fought to stay together for about two months (threats of restraining order from parents, her not being allowed to contact me). She ended up breaking it off because she knew her family wouldn't accept. I miss her very much. She has gone on a "boy crazy" social media rampage now, soon after we finished. She was never open about us, and that's what ruined our ending. She's throwing shade at me and making it seem as though I'm the one who did her wrong. Now we don't communicate at all and she took me off all social media. I know I'm not the one who mistreated her. I never gave up on us, she did. I'm stuck between letting go and holding on. I know the person she's fronting to be right now, is not the real her. But she is fighting so hard to suppress the same sex feelings, that she feels she must show off boy drama. I want to move on and stop hurting, because I feel I'm the only one left feeling hurt to the extent that I do. I still would not post anything anywhere near that would hurt her feelings, but she deliberately does. I only want to believe everything she said about us and our future, when we were okay. Before she came out and everything changed forever.

Dear Anonymous

I can understand how hard it must have been for you, to have a best friend of four years turn into someone you can't identify. It's like everything you once thought was real, is now something you couldn't explain to anyone, because it wouldn't make sense. I know you said "same sex" but there's no difference, when it comes to love, none of that matters. People will take that and run with it and never want to date the same sex again, due to the pain from who hurt them. Never feel ashamed of who you love and why you love them, I want you to take this situation as a lesson you were meant to learn in your life. Your best friend wasn't meant to travel this far in life with you, she wasn't meant to grow with who you're going to be, because who she is now, will forever be. We sometimes over analyze why people leave, was it us, was it them, truth is, doesn't matter who's at fault, just be thankful you let go, because one day you'll be grateful for being let go of. Sometimes we need to let people go because we use love as an excuse, to not see the dishonest love, silent judgements, and people who give up so quickly, never loved you as much as they lead you to believe.

People don't just walk out your life when they love you. I believe connections you can't save, were meant to break, we never think about letting people go when we meet them, when we fall in love with them, if you overanalyzed every connection you made, a mess would be made, you might never love them, but in this situation, you were meant to. I truly believe you cross paths with people who were meant to show us a part of us we never knew was there. The kind that felt love in letting go, and letting people we once loved, free, and becoming a better you.

Anonymous 12

My boyfriend of 3 years and I ended 8 months ago, we still live together. The first month he tried getting back together (I was milking it) he told me "we owe it to ourselves" and for him, it'll always be me. He hung with his friends and 24 hours later decided he didn't want me. It's been a huge fight ever since. I'm still here because I believe he's my soulmate. I know he's not himself right now, I know deep down he loves me and still cares, but he's the kind of person that shuts down because the pain is too much. I know it's time I let go, but I know he's my soul mate.

Dear Anonymous

I hope you don't take this wrong, but just because you believe he's your soulmate, is not a reason to stick around. If he's truly your soulmate, let him go and God will bring you two together if it's meant to be. The more you try and fight what's already written, the more unhappy you both will be. I believe in timing of all, I believe that people can be right for each other, but the timing could be wrong. I also believe signs people show you, if they keep repeating the same mistakes and treating you like you're not worth an explanation, they're showing how their worth doesn't amount to yours. We all believe someone is our soulmate when we truly love them, we fight for them even when we shouldn't have to. You shouldn't have to make someone see how much you love them, they should know. They should feel it. But at the end of the day, not even love is enough to hold together a broken bond. Sometimes people just let go mentally and hold onto you physically because they don't want you to find the one, you're meant for, they believe holding you back will always keep you. But you need to understand, when they do this, they have complete control over you and that's where you need to really think about what you're allowing, because it will always continue if you let it. Sometimes you need to let go and see what really is meant to happen, or who's really meant for you out there.

Anonymous 13

I'm a 25-year old single parent. I was with the father of my children for 5 years, and within those years he cheated on me constantly and abused me emotionally and mentally. When I finally ended things, I created a shell of the person I was, and that was 5 years ago, I haven't dated since. I joined the army national guard a year ago and I met some lifelong friends. Those friends brought me out of my shell and helped me find myself again. Last September, I returned home from basic training. I had to report to drill that following weekend. There I met the guy who I eventually fell in love with. I never noticed him at first but when I finally talked to him and looked him in the eyes, I had a gut feeling. It was like a warning. Something told me that he would change my life, but I didn' t know if it would be a good or bad way. I took the risk and we started hanging out. We hung out 5 times before I told him I was attracted to him. He was so easy to talk to. I knew I could trust him with anything. We ended up being best friends, but so much more. I never had a connection so deep with anyone else. We were like an unofficial couple. A month into everything I told him I was in love with him. A couple days before he told me he was falling for me, but he was scared because he didn' t think he was good enough. Things were good, yet he was still confused. He told me there was no one else, that I was his **main** girl. He was everything I wanted in a guy. He was affectionate, caring, funny, driven, and spontaneous. The one thing we argued about was the title, he never would define the relationship, always said he wasn' t "ready to love anyone" . I noticed him changing a week before he stopped talking to me. The night before I caught him with another girl, but I had no right to say anything. He was not mine. Up to this day, he still doesn' t know I already knew. He just stopped talking to me. I was a mess. The one person I honestly thought would never walk out on me, did. Three weeks later, I reached out to him and he said he is sorry. I asked him why, and he said it was getting too real and he was scared. We talked things out and we agreed on being just friends. We talked here and there but it was nothing like before. He was seeing someone. It stung for a bit, until a month of them being together he told her the same things. A month later, he is engaged, the news broke my heart. He told me he wasn't ready for anything serious, yet he put a ring on someone else's finger. I was happy for him, but at the same time I was heartbroken. Two weeks into the new year, he calls me out of the blue, and wants to catch up and to get closure, I invited him to my house to talk. I told him how bad he hurt me and a part of me will always love him. He asked me what I wanted. We tried to be just friends, something we never were. I told him I wanted more but he was still scared. Back track, when he showed up to my home, he didn't have a ring on. They were promise rings since she lives in Texas for college. He told me it didn't work out, the long distance was too much, I believed him. After spilling everything I needed to say, we had sex. I stopped it. I believed him and I let him in again only to find out they were still together. And he only had sex with me to satisfy his needs. I reached out to his girlfriend and told her what happened. They are still together. And he is still cheating on her. A couple days ago I texted him, because it was his son's birthday, and I wanted to give him best wishes. I have not heard from him since. After four years, I decide to put myself out there, to start dating again only for it to slap me in the face. I believe he did want to be with me, but he was scared being with someone who loves him for who he truly is, the person he doesn't show the world. He can't deny the chemistry. He can't deny his feelings. But he fights them. It hurts still. It hurts every day.

Dear Anonymous

I want to start off by saying, the more you allow, the more they'll continue hurting you. You learned a lot from the first time you were with the father of your children, you learned what it felt like, to basically have your heart ripped out your chest. You finally left and decided to find you. But did you completely find yourself? Because old habits seem to come back fast and if you let them repeat, you can't blame anyone but yourself. Your worth is so much more than your love for someone who only treats you less than that. There are people out who only meant to teach you a lesson in life, and love, and it seems like you have met two of them. When you meet someone who you instantly fall in love with, it feels great, you feel nothing you felt before. It's easy to fall in love, especially with someone who's good at faking. I learned a lot about love and relationships, even friendships, to know toxic people have a way of showing you all their good and hiding the phony parts of them, until it's impossible. Once you see the side of someone you never saw before, you need to accept its who they are, who they always were. Don't make excuses why someone loved you, or whether they still do. You can't tell yourself how they feel, nor will you ever get an answer directly from them. Toxic people will always intoxicate the people they aren't meant to be with. The more you keep fighting this, the more pain you bring upon yourself and you end up drowning in it. Toxic people have a way with words, and no actions, they're also good with showing you nothing at all, making you into a complete fool. What I'm trying to say, the universe will never match you with someone who's hard to love. If it's hard to be with someone, it's a sign you've reached the end of the road, and it's time to move on.

Anonymous 14

I recently broke up with someone who I felt drained me. They didn't cheat or anything domestically, I just felt like I was giving someone more than what I was receiving. After I broke up with him, I immediately experienced an awakening happen over a period of three weeks, and I'm still going through it. Not only has my soul and energy changed, I feel as though I'm channeling a completely new life, outlook, and energy. Nonetheless, I had time to reflect, and my previous relationship also provided insights on areas of growth, in regards, to moving forward, I've been pondering lately on my poor behavior and understanding I was at fault in areas due to my struggle with showing emotion. And even lacking certain emotions, now with trying to understand myself in previous situations and learn from them, I struggle. I can't tell if it was wrong for me to get in the relationship in the first place, because it wasn't necessarily what I wanted, or looked at it as growth and opportunity to see things about myself I never saw, but he pointed out. I saw a quote that said, "some boys are meant to prepare you for your man" and that kind of resonated with me. Now, this new situation comes about and this time while I am going through my awakening and the signs pulling me in this new direction. This new situation feels right, no hesitation in my mind. I feel like I'm at a point of surrender. I want something different. A different life, opportunity, and I feel like I am jumping into something. I believe my purpose is to see beauty in people that may not see it in themselves. By the time they realize it, after however long our encounter, my time ends, and they feel like they are in love, causing me to wander. I'm seeing more of that. Every person who was in my life, they always told me I gave them something they will never find again. It's concerning for me. I feel like a wanderer.

Dear Anonymous

To me, you seem very strong, I haven't heard many stories on how "I realized" it's always "what to do" but I can tell you've grown, and I don't even know you. And you state you don't really do love? When I read that, all I could feel was love. We all give our all to someone and wish we could un-live and not feel everything. Everyone you meet has a purpose in your life and sometimes they live that purpose, and if they were not meant to stick around, they always go, and sometimes we never understand their true purpose, but try and grow with that much. Never be afraid to love again, after being broken, or left on the edge, someone out there is ready for someone like you, to love them and be their person. Love is the most beautiful feeling I've ever witnessed. I don't know why I ever thought terribly of it. But it took a lot of misunderstandings, halfway love, and accepting comfort instead of what I deserved. You learn the hard way, love is beautiful, but that's the beauty in it. You get to appreciate real love when you learn the heart break of it all. I can admit to being toxic in situations, but I never made anyone feel less than what I think of them, I never let anyone I loved, feel alone. Only you will truly understand, without the clouded judgement of others. I'm all about accepting every part of me, we all have demons, neither the same, but I do agree, anyone who is toxic, should face that, and come to terms with loving who they are without hurting another.

To get people to stay, that were only meant to
wander, aren' t people you should fight for.
You will love, but please, don' t confuse love,
with the lust of wanting to feel love. The void
you keep trying to fill will forever be empty
fighting for ones, who only poison your heart.

People who come in your life, who were only meant to wander, in other words, someone who wasn't meant to stay.

You outgrow a lot of situations, and people you grow loving, not everyone you connect with will be a lifelong connection.

People were meant to come in and out your life for reasons, you can't un-live those times, but you can accept they outlived that time.

I' m mature enough to admit
I held some toxic traits
and how I let myself be consumed by you.

I' m mature enough to admit
I wasn' t perfect,
I know I brought pain too.

Anonymous 15

I met someone I thought I was so in love with and would be together forever, but he constantly kept cheating one me, then became verbal and physical abuse. Even being pregnant with his child, nothing mattered. I'm not a saint, but I tried everything I could to do, to be the one he needed, but he wanted more. Now my son and I escaped a toxic relationship and are better than ever. It was hard leaving someone I "loved" but letting go was one of the decisions I ever made. I am now an independent mother who will never be that sad old girl ever again.

Dear Anonymous

It's comforting knowing you grew apart from the bad, you left all the burden behind you. Now you are looking towards a happier, positive life, full of blessings. You grow to realize the "love" you once had was not a that's true, it was a way of getting you ready for your soul mate, to learn what love isn't, so you may love indefinitely. Love yourself first, always. Sometimes you never know when it's time to walk away, until being separated from the situation feels better than it ever did while you were in it.

Anonymous 16

I was in a three-year relationship. I got dumped with in November, started working things out again in January then he decided in February, he "cannot give me what I want". Few days later I had a gut feeling he was dating someone else, I acted out of character to find out if it was true, and he admitted to it, saying he "used me" and was "lonely" and I was "all he knew". I still love him. However, I know I can never go back because I would never be able to trust him from this point on. Just wish I could stop thinking about him I am taking the time to work on my mental health and overall the best version of myself.

Dear Anonymous,

I have told many people this, including myself, no one who is ready to go when it's convenient, is someone you should continue holding closely to your heart. Someone who makes loving them a contest. You should never have to worry about the one you love. You should never have to try and make them stay every time they try to go, people should not be hard to keep, or hard to hold them close when they want so desperately to walk. Never over think why they did you wrong, or why they left. Focus on what you did to keep what's left, together. And work on loving yourself, so you know exactly how to accept love from another.

Anonymous 17

I' ve been bullied by some of my classmates. I refused to see them, it' s the reason behind my absences. I don' t know what I did for them to hate me, all I know is I never did anything to harm someone or putting someone down. I express my feelings through writing also but it' s kinda private. I have no self-esteem because I know all I get is negative feedback from them. They' re all insensitive to the point that they' re slowly killing me. This is the worst experience I' ve ever experienced.

Dear Anonymous,

I can relate to this on an intimate level. In high school, I was shy, and I didn' t have many friends because of bullying. People would call me the girl who "didn' t talk" some disrespected me, and some would use me being quiet, as a way, to talk down on me. Back then I was scared, I never did anything for anyone to bother me, but I tried not to let them get to me. My senior year, I had two freshman girls call me "ugly" because I was friends with a friend of theirs, I' m guessing they didn' t approve of that, so they wanted to fight me because I was "ugly". It was pure humor to me. I started writing a lot in high school. I realized how silly it was to judge me on my physical appearance because they were upset. I had a girl sleep with a guy I was dating because she thought she had control over him, walked up to my face and told me, but joke was on her, I didn't do anything with him, and I didn't care, she made herself look stupid. I guess it's easier to look back now and see all the things happened to me. You grow a lot and you learn they only pick you apart because they feel at a low point in their life. I've known people who died because of bullying, because they took their own life. Don't let anyone make you believe you're not worthy, and beautiful. Your beauty is within you, and your heart.

Anonymous 18

I just want to say thank you, from the bottom of my heart, you didn't directly message me or give me advice, but your words do wonders. They are able, to heal broken hearts from across the world. Able to ease the mind of someone overthinking in a completely different state. When you had an open dm night where we got the opportunity to message you a story of something toxic in our lives, I typed the paragraph at least five times, and cried each time but never had the strength to send it. I was scared. Scared to put it out there in the world because when it was behind closed doors it stayed there in the dark. Today, that person came home every night and day, yelled at me and called me horrible names, decide to follow me then message me. They told me about a family member who's taking advantage of them and just vented. Like the good person I am, I gave them comfort and advice. And in the end, they tried to stay "friends" while flirting, telling me they had a new girl already, just being disrespectful, but thanks to you, I wiped away the tears, gathered my strength, and stood my ground. I said no and went off in the most respectful yet peaceful way possible. Today, I let go of someone who had my voice and feelings in chains. I let go of someone who mentally abused me and took me for granted for a year. Please keep writing, thank you.

Dear Anonymous

This was a beautiful message, my heart dropped. It's touching, knowing my words really have so much influence. So beautiful to know they help heal others, not just myself. You're a beautiful soul, thank you for reaching out to me. I'm very sorry you had to go through something like that, I'm sorry you could never find someone to love you, the way you give love, but that is how we learn who is for us, by finding out the ones who aren't. That's the saddest part about love, you get confused so many times, blinded by what your heart lusts. You don't deserve any heartache that comes your way, and you must understand to fully believe it. You have a good heart, so to be matched with someone who could only speak on having one, but showed the opposite, you don't deserve a love that was a mirage in the first place, just only to you, and as much as that makes you feel a fool, you're still worth more than you believe. Your heart is incredible, and the way you love is out of this world, it can be the greatest or worst thing that could ever happen, but you will become broken only to become the soul you were meant to be, along with the soul who fits with you. Keep growing from the hurt, the pain, and everything you felt from that time. Focus on you, the love you have for yourself, and why you let go of the misery, and found the love inside you.

Anonymous 19

To make a very long story short, I've been in this off and on toxic situationship, for about a year in a half. It honestly has become like a love triangle the way he goes back and forth between me and his ex. I'm just emotionally, mentally, and physically drained from dealing with all of this. Yet I continue to put up with it, out of loneliness. It's horrible that I do this to myself, I clearly don't know my worth.

Dear Anonymous

I have said this before, but what you allow will always continue. What you accept, will be taken as it's okay to keep doing. You need to set aside your heart, from what needs to be. Someone who just walks in and out of your life does not have anything but misery coming your way. The vibes from them alone will bring you misery. There's no love in someone who's only around to use you and take advantage of the good heart you have. You stay and continue to go back because you're lonely, then come back when there's nowhere to go, it sounds like you're both in it for the wrong reasons. You can't label it love, if they're only around to keep you from being lonely, you can't expect to be treated anything more than you accept. Just because you believe you deserve better, you don't become better until you learn to let go, of the things that blind you from wasting your heart on someone who doesn't even care to listen to the beat.

Anonymous 20

What should you do, if a guy suddenly falls away from you because they don't want to pull you down with them, and they don't want to interrupt what you have going?

Dear Anonymous

If someone tells you they can't be with you for reasons because of them, believe them, they need to work on them in order to love you, like you deserve. Stop searching for someone, let the universe present them you. Search for who you are and find who you are, before you try to give your love away.

Don't let anyone distract you
from being the best version of you.
No one can be you, like you,
OWN THAT.

List (5) things you need to work on:

1) _____

2) _____

3) _____

4) _____

5) _____

Often, we let others convince us
we're not worthy of an opinion on ourselves.

Often, we let others convince us
We're not worthy.

Anonymous 21

I currently feel like I love this guy who can't give me a title. I'm always just "his friend" when I meet his friends. I do everything for this guy, buy him things, give him money, always go to him. When I ask about the title, he says he "likes the way things are" I met him about three years ago, when I was 19 and I am now 22, and he is about to be 30. When I first met him, I was unaware he had a gf, I ended up fighting the girl and still talking to him. I lost my two best friends over him, I drink a lot because of him, and ultimately have lost myself. Everyone tells me he talks to other girls, they even come tell me. But I can't seem to let go. I recently saw this girl he talked to is going to Europe which coincidentally he is too. But I can't stand up or even give him an ultimatum. He never gave me anything but heartaches, yet I insist to stay there and be used. He makes me feel unworthy, no matter what I do it's not enough for him to even say we are dating. I'm not sure what to do. I can't let go and I don't know why.

Dear Anonymous

See, me reading that, all I immediately think is "wow it doesn't seem like it would be hard to leave" but the more I read, the more I feel everything deeply. I can say your first problem, is that fact "you gave him everything" and only

explained material things, that didn't make you
question why he "liked the way things were"
because you need the validation of a title, he uses
that against you, makes you want it and he knows
that is how he keeps you, by faking it like he wants
all of you, but only wants what he wants, and gets
he wants elsewhere. You need to realize, what you
give out is not always beneficial to your own being,
the more you give, the more you become blind because
of all the love you give trying to get in return.
Whatever good you got out of the situation is long
gone, and you know it, you said it, you just now
need to put it into perspective and leave. You keep
hurting yourself holding on, and this is the game he
was playing the whole time, it's time to win.

Anonymous 22

I met a guy 6 months ago he was the sweetest
thing. Fed me, took care of me when I was sick,
always wanted me around. Told me he loved me. He was
a college student in Cali (where I reside) he's
from New Jersey, so he would leave for holiday
breaks and come back. He started talking to me about
his "best friend" which is his ex gf, saying how
they were engaged at one point and she always
thought he was cheating when he wasn't. We were
intimate since I met him. Almost every day. I soon
found out they were on and off, but I was too in
love to care or to let go. He started treating me
less like he didn't love me anymore, as months have
gone by school is finished and he is back with her
in New Jersey and I am 7 weeks pregnant with his
child which he knows and basically told me he

doesn' t know if he wants to be in the child's life. His gf is pregnant too. He blocked my number and blocked me on social media. My heart is crushed, and I know this is something I'll never get over.

Dear Anonymous

    I'm so sorry you had to deal with someone who's heartless. I'm sorry you're carrying a child through such misery. I pray your pregnancy stays healthy and the stress doesn't hurt you or the baby. It's the scariest thing, giving your all away to someone and expecting them to give it to you in return. You'll never know until it is too late, when feelings already resonated, and you are deep in. You'll love the worst kinds of hearts throughout your lifetime but one thing for sure is you love these people for a reason, and you'll have a purpose in their life, as they will in yours. The way this works, not everyone is someone, who's meant to stay, when the bad takes itself out the story, you need to stop blaming yourself. You need to stop thinking it was your fault such tragedy happened, which was never you're doing in the first place. You gave all of you, you showed up, gave way more than you received. Remember those times, remember the times you loved and did everything for them, because those are the most important. Not their character, not the way they treated you. You will always end up exactly where they want you by hoarding pain, they left you with. Never run from the signs when you know you saw them, accept sometimes people disappear from your life, only for a blessing to appear. The universe will never take something away from you, without giving you

something much more beautiful. Let go, what is gone.
Never change your heart because you lessen your
worth for someone who doesn' t know theirs.

Speak it into existence,

I love _____
about myself the most.

The longer I kept toxicity surrounding me, the more I let it consume me.
I created my own toxic traits.
I became my own worst enemy when I kept loving what was destroying me.
I used love as an excuse.
I learned love isn' t pain, but you' ll go through a lot of pain to understand.

Anonymous 23

My boyfriend had this female friend he used to "mess around" with before me. He does not speak with her or anything of the sort. But recently, he posted on snapchat videos of his brother's dog and she commented on them. I feel a bit insecure about her randomly commenting, and it just makes me feel some type of way. I did bring it to his attention, but he just assures me there's nothing to worry about. For the past two days I've been having reoccurring nightmares with her in them. I don't know what to do. I'm unsure what I want, and unsure what I deserve. To feel insecure about a girl from his past, I just want to not care about her at all.

Dear Anonymous,

In my opinion, it's a bit wrong to have past lovers, regardless of the situation, on your social media following them when you're "nothing" it never made much sense to me, but sometimes your trust with your partner should have more power than that. If he assures you have no problem, believe him, but don't turn a blind eye to her or the situation. If you keep seeing it happen a lot, then I would question whether it's something or not. Don't think too much and beat yourself up over something that really could be nothing.

Anonymous 24

It's one of those nights for me, which is becoming so frequent, I feel so empty. I miss him. I miss the life I once had. He took everything I could feel. I just want to be at peace, and I know I can only find it in myself, but I feel so alone.

Dear Anonymous,

Unfortunately, the pain will always feel like you're nothing, and can't breathe. It may take years to heal fresh wounds. It doesn't matter how long it lasted, if you have a good heart, the way you love is always deep and the pain is always unbearable. You need to feel everything and come to an understanding that you will feel that forever, or you can try to find happiness in places it does exist.

Anonymous 25

Well, he left me, out of nowhere. He told me he wanted to be by himself so he could work on himself and focus on work, but immediately got with someone else. It's been a month and some days are worse than others. We were together for almost two years. We had our fair share of arguments but nothing I thought we couldn't overcome. Everything was okay before it happened, although I did feel a difference in him days before. Our relationship was good, although he had already done me wrong leading

me to become so insecure. I felt like I was the
problem. I couldn' t keep him in love with me. No
effort put into getting my things back even when he
has time. My possessions are truly the only thing
that will give us the chance to meet again. After
that, there will be reason to be in each other' s
lives.

Dear Anonymous,

No one will just leave out of nowhere.
There' s always a reason, they will know but you
might not. People don' t just wake up one day and
decide they don' t want you anymore, they have
thought about it, many times, trying to find ways to
leave. I believe sometimes no answer is the answer
people find most comfort in. Knowing they won' t
have to explain how they feel or explain why they
left, they' ll move on and forget it happened. There
was love but it wasn' t enough to stay. Love is
strong but sometimes it' s not enough when it comes
to an end, when it' s over, it' s over. If you stay
away, you' ll feel like you never know what could
have happened. If you decide to go back, you wonder
what things could have been. And you' re scared if
you go back nothing will ever feel the same, and
you' re right, everything will feel foreign and new.
In that instance, change isn' t something you want,
but right now you are giving him the power. If you
truly believe love exists within this, I would give
you the best of prayers. If you believe you deserve
someone who will love you, just as much as you love,
I would say this is just the beginning. You don' t
have to hurt forever, or wait for him, let him know

how you feel one last time and let that determine
how the rest will go.

Note to self,

People will use your mental illness as a weapon,
not understanding how weak it makes you.
They'll bully you until you hit your breaking
point, then pray for you when you've hit rock
bottom. It's hard being strong in a world with
people trying to turn you against yourself.

Your
Mental health is important.
Take care of you.

Never second guess giving someone a compliment.

If you' re thinking it, express it to them, you never know if they may need it.

You could change their whole day.

You're searching for more and wanting more, after
those long years you deserve more.
Don't settle because you have history,
that's the worst thing to do.
If you're not being treated like you deserve,
and nothing is being reciprocated,
don't stick around.

Some people you meet
are just a part
of your road to self-discovery,
don' t let everyone
have such a hold over your heart.

Vent Below.

_____

_____

_____

_____

_____

_____

_____

_____

_____

_____

People will stay in relationships they outgrew and expect happiness to come from it, nothing good comes from something that's no longer in the cards. The more you force, the more the relationship becomes toxic on both ends. One see's the other already walked away emotionally, but decides to fight because they love them, and the other decides to hold onto them because they don't want to hurt them yet search for attention elsewhere. This ends in pain, which could be resolved with communication. **A word of advice**: if you're not happy, let your partner know, because they're aware, but are holding on because you're confusing them. The pain you will bring upon them will overcome, but the longer you hold them close the more toxic the relationship becomes. I don't believe toxicity just comes in physical abuse. I believe the biggest toxicity comes from mistreating yourself which creates toxicity in the one you love or wish to set free. Always playing victim doesn't make you a good person, especially if you can't be accountable. You can't be scared to let someone go because you don't want to hurt them. You're hurting them more by holding on knowing you don't love them anymore.

Write a letter to someone you let go:

_____

_____

_____

_____

_____

_____

_____

_____

_____

_____

_____

_____

_____

Anonymous 26

I've been struggling a lot with accepting my emotions (mostly anger) for what they are, and not try to change them. Just saw your tweet asking what we'd like to hear about, and if you have advice or words on this, I would deeply cherish it. I love your tweets and oftentimes send them to me privately as well so I can go back later and feed my inner strength and peace. Thank you for everything you do.

Dear Anonymous,

Struggling with your emotions is by one of the hardest things I've come to realize, along from trying to control your heart. We feel different emotions for reasons we might not understand, but they're written into our lives for reasons, reasons that make sense, just not to us. We don't want to hate someone we've once loved, but sometimes we feel anger towards them because of the pain they brought upon us. It's unbearable at the least, but you need to face your emotions head on, and try to make sense of them. Make sense of the situation and try and understand your feelings. Feel what you feel whether you like it or not, you don't have a choice sometimes, your heart reacts without demand and makes it harder. But accept when you feel mad or sad, it's the same as being happy. You can't feel one emotion for the rest of your life, that's why we have many, to be able to not hoarder the same old emotions on old pain, accept you can't change people and sometimes we have to let ones we love go for reasons that won't ever make sense. Just know, it's not meant to serve you anymore purpose, let the demons go along with that.

Anonymous 27

My entire life my mom and dad were abusive mentally and physically, in high school, I met my soul mate, best friend, other half, and everything. Before our senior year we got in a bad car accident and he passed away, it's been so hard without him. I tried to be in relationships, and I can't because the love he gave me. I have yet, come in contact with someone, so loving and caring and I know I'll never find him in anyone I stopped comparing him to people, but now I just can't stop wondering if I'll ever love or be loved again with abundance. I pray you give me hope because I love your writing. I love you, thank you for doing what you do because the things you have said are the things I could never get out.

Dear Anonymous

Wow, I'm so sorry for your loss. I can say I do come from an understanding view. I also lost someone who was a soulmate of mine, and it's far from easy to "move on". It's impossible honestly. The only thing that really happens is you'll start to accept you never see their face again but will always feel their spirit. They're still with you every day, more than ever. And that is the hardest part to accept, because we're selfish when it comes to contact with others. I was very selfish, I wanted her back and it broke me even more. What I can say,

is pray. Pray every day, the ones you love stay
healthy and happy. As for the grieving process, it
takes time. It takes a lot of crying yourself to
sleep, to being happy to instantly depressed. We' re
human, we are an emotional roller coaster. Death is
so terrifying and losing someone who' s so close to
your heart is the worst thing to have to live with.
But know they love you, when you' re just thinking
of them know they' re looking down on you, proud you
made it this far. And for love, yes you' ll find
someone who will pick up the pieces, it might not be
for a while, or could be when you let it. You just
have to let them in, it' s okay to guard your heart
a bit, but don' t be scared to love another because
the love you had got taken from you, that love you
once had, will forever remain within you, and your
heart. And they will bring you someone who will love
you, just believe.

We stay because we love hard.
When we put our hearts all in, there's no taking
the love back. We manipulate our hearts to believe
if we felt love, it's love. We're taught to hold
close anyone who made us feel love.

The same comfort they gave felt like home.
We condition our hearts to think we need their love
since we've been dependent on it, never thought it
would be possible to live without. We stay, hoping
one day they'll love us back. We love too hard,
making it hard to be loved in return.

We chase and chase, until we realize their love
isn't a anything to gain, when they treat yours
like a game. Knowing our worth is far more than what
we're accepting yet consuming less because we
don't believe we're good enough.

Mental health days are so important.

Spending time in your own solitude,
doesn' t mean your depressed or antisocial,
some days you just need a break
from the world and be away from everyone.
This goes for school, work, friends, family.

There' s nothing wrong with that.

I know you think it's wrong to feel you can't
be friends with someone because their energy
brings you down. You're not wrong.
You can't spread positivity
while being friends with the enemy,
some people will never grow
but that doesn't mean you have to suffer too.

You grow up learning how to treat others,
how to love others unconditionally.
All these years you grew up learning,
while missing the most important lesson,
how to love yourself.

Why does it take years to be taught that?

Anonymous 28

Hey Sara! I hope you're doing well! I've really been enjoying your messages and quotes and wanted to ask you for some advice. I see you're successful and that's great! But I know with success also comes people who don't like your book or the art that you put out. I'm really struggling with being confident in continuing to put my own art out in public due to fear of rejection and harsh criticism.

I wanted to ask,

how you get through the harsh words or rejection?
What drives you to keep going if you fail?

Dear Anonymous:

I was very insecure, in the past, when it came to sharing my work with the world, mainly because it came from somewhere deep inside the depths of my heart and soul, and to share that with the world scared me and that's because some humans are judgmental. I hated judgement. I loathed the feeling of not being accepted for who I am, and the decisions I chose to make because of who I was. I'm human too, so it hurt to think I could be misunderstood, or the pressure of keeping it real could hurt someone to, scared me tremendously. It wasn't until the years recently I started to not care much what others thought of me, to live more freely within the vibrance of myself because the light I brought shined over so many others. I started inspiring others through my journey, and it became something beautiful, knowing my story could save some the heartache, the healing. It's a different kind of love seeing compliments, and how others feel from my work. I received a lot of amazing feedback, to the point when I received one bad review, I became confused. I was hurt, but I had to come to understanding my story won't fit with others the way I felt it. I had to understand not everyone is going to be a fan or admire my work. Some are still letting toxicity consume them, so my happiness was darkness to them. Some are still healing, so my happiness was too much for them. See, I already grew from the dark times, even though I spoke on a lot from my past, my overall aura spoke what some couldn't relate to. My work isn't for everyone, or the right time for everyone. But for the one's my work has touched. To heal, inspire, so many souls the best part of my success. I no longer take bad reviews or harsh words to heart I just pray for the souls behind them. I was once lost too, so I totally understand. But above all, I don't write for anyone but myself, writing has been my therapy since 2010. Whether it inspires some, that's a gift. But no one's words will ever make me fail, because this heart I have is incredibly big, so I won't ever stop sharing that love.

I' ve learned,
love is such a scary place to be,
if you' re not exactly sure
you' re ready to be there.
As I look now and see
how love is one of my biggest fears.
Because I' ve given someone all of me,
loved them with my whole heart
and it will didn' t work.

Anonymous 29

I haven' t spoken about this in a while. I
still cry about it sometimes. Two years ago, I got
an abortion and I don' t think I fully healed from
it (emotionally). There are times when I find myself
sad. I still feel guilt. I wouldn' t say regretful.
But I just haven' t felt the same since. And I think
that feeling of guilt towards myself and how much I
beat myself up, rolled into the relationship I just
got out of. I poured so much of myself into him and
he didn' t give it back in return. He left me
because he said I was "too much" for him. I' m
still sad about that too.

Anonymous 30

I'd like to see you write about forgiving
the person who broke your heart completely, who
never looked back or apologized. (That's what
happened to me just a few weeks ago by someone I've
been with for 3 years now, he just left with the
girl he cheated with, without even breaking it off,

it killed me. How do I forgive this person? How do I
set myself free Sara?

Dear Anonymous

Forgiving someone who completely torn your
heart a part is one of the hardest things to do,
because well, you invested so much time and energy
into this human. Your heart invested so much love in
them. It's going to hurt for a while because of the
fact they decided to go ghost instead of speaking
the love they no longer feel. What hurts the heart
most isn't all the love it gave, but the rejection
of not feeling like our love was good enough. What
hurts the most is being let go of someone you shared
your deepest secrets, dreams, and soul with. It's
the realization you never were meant to last. It
scars. Forgiveness will be the last thing on your
mind. You may think of how to be spiteful, how to
create jealously, you may place yourself out to be a
fool because of the love you hold that's only
within you now. Getting your heart completely broken
can result into completely losing you, if you
aren't careful. The one thing you should never do,
is compare yourself to who they chose over you,
instead, focus on the road that's ended and now how
to rebuild yourself from this block in your journey.
Forgiveness will come, but first, you'll see how
self-reflection is something you need to practice.
So many of us blame ourselves for someone deciding
to walk away, when our hearts never done them wrong,
but sometimes the universe has different plans for
you. Sometimes the path your taking isn't meant to
be forever. Sometimes you grow and you confuse that
with heartache. What you need to become Intune with,

it's okay to grow from things you once held closely to your heart, or still do, and to learn to let those things free, because they no longer hold that same purpose in your life. It's okay to take your time when it comes to forgiveness, because to forgive them for damaging your heart, you need to forgive yourself for allowing them to.

Anonymous 31

I just need someone to talk to, what do you do when someone physically and mentally hurts you, but you still can't help but be madly in love with them? You wanted your person to be him? I know I am an idiot for thinking this and feeling this way.

Dear Anonymous

There's no love there, on their end. The love is within you only, and at this point, the love is what you've created in your head and it sounds like you're in love with the idea of love, and they aren't the right kind of love you deserve.
Let go and find the love you deserve.

Anonymous 32

For years I've tried my hardest to be what this guy wanted. I did anything and everything for him and constantly assumed that if I did this one thing, he'd realize how much I cared for him. After countless nights of me wondering why I'm not enough or why he couldn't just open his eyes, I decided to give up, not because I didn't care anymore, but because he didn' t. Every time I tried to become strong enough and tell myself I' m worthy and deserve better, I find myself wishing it was him instead of whatever guy I' m with. I guess you could say I accept what I think I deserve, even though I know better, but can' t get myself to believe it. Here I am, still stuck and waiting for the magical day that he decides I am enough. Trying to let go but can' t.

Dear Anonymous

Where you went wrong, was when you knew better but chose to stay, nothing good comes from staying where you' re not wanted. I was once that girl who was vulnerable enough to believe I could make someone love me. I once thought if I waited, our time would come. I believed in timing, and that two people who were meant for each other, would make their way back to each other if that' s what the universe meant. But today, I don' t see time. I see blessings, and that if someone doesn' t love me in that moment, love won' t grow. I was that girl who stayed, who played the fool, for trust me, I know nothing good comes from waiting. If your time wasn' t that time, don' t waste your time waiting for them to love you, because they won' t, or they might, but turn out nothing good for you. That' s the biggest lesson I learned when it came to love, what' s not meant for you won' t ever be right for you.

Anonymous 33

I've been struggling with loving myself because I was told I'm all these amazing things, but I'm not "intellectually stimulating". This is something I've never been through before. I've been struggling my whole life to love myself (currently on a 110-pound weight loss journey and only 20 to my goal weight) I loved myself before I was told this. In a world where I base so much of my self-worth on what I can give to others, this has been a kick in the teeth. Can you write about self-worth and the power of our words?

Dear Anonymous

The power of words, the fact they could destroy you, or give you the power to go harder. You'll meet people who will have opinions on your every move. Some will judge your appearance, your character, and your overall self, they will paint their illusion and run with it. But listen, just because they view you the way they do, doesn't mean you let it define you. You can't let someone who doesn't live through what you go through, tell who you are, or what you should feel about yourself. Beauty comes in form of physical, but also within, and that's the kind of beauty that matters when it comes down to it. The beauty you hold within your heart, is the beauty that lasts until you are no longer in human form, but also carries on with your spirit. Physical beauty will fade with time, because

we all grow old, we all through stress, and many
other things that impact the outlook on ourselves.
As long, as your healthy, happy, and loved by you,
that should be your only concern. Don' t hold other
opinions on you make your vision of you blurry, your
view is the only view that can be threatened.

Anonymous 34

I feel like the last year of my life was one
that' s almost impossible to sum up. I lived with my
girlfriend at the time, who was "straight. " We
fell in love with who we were, not for a gender. She
was my best friend. She was my world. She called me
"her person" and she was mine. We both are
Christian (she introduced me back to my faith in
God), never once thought it would be the reason we
ended. Her family was starting to catch on and her
"secret" of being in a relationship with a girl.
so instead of her taking my hand as just a friend
she decided cheating on me was the best option. She
went from being my best friend to being with this
guy and has said the most terrible lies about me
just to protect her sexual identity. She hid me as a
friend for two months and then blocked me. Nobody
recognizes her anymore. Some of her last words to me
came with tears, saying "you know this isn' t what
I want" , as if she was saying she was only doing
this relationship with a guy to prove something and
that she will always love me. The way she left my
life, blocked me randomly, tells disgusting lies
just because she thinks she' s protecting her
identity ... I have had to defend who I am for the
last year from a person I would never hurt. I see
her around because we play soccer and still go to

church, but no words are said I just want closure. I just want to understand how she can do what she has done. Does she believe her own lies? Did she even love me? I have spent the last year waiting like a fool. Thinking she'll come around. My heart drops still when I see her and holding back tears is nearly impossible. I just want to tell her I love her, and I wish it was different. How I'd go back just to say goodbye if I knew the last time, I saw her. How I would have held a hug a little longer or just told her to smile and laugh and live life and be happy. I wish I could just hold her hand one more time and remind her that I'd never be her enemy. She has lost sight of who she is, she looks at me like I'm a villain, it's sad. It's so much more than what I'm trying to sum up. It hurts and I lay at night reading poems and wondering if she ever just wants to pick up the phone and talk to me. She was my world, still is, just in the worst way.

Dear Anonymous

_____

_____

_____

_____

_____

_____

_____

_____

_____

_____

_____

It's so beautiful seeing people happy,
and self-love's written all over them.
I think it's beautiful
when someone's growing into the soul
they're meant to bloom into.
Self-love will always be
the *most important lesson* in your story.

Anonymous 35

I've been in a relationship for 7 years and 8 months, and finally decided to break up with my boyfriend last month on the 17th of March. Obviously not all 7 years has been hell there was a few beautiful years too, but at the end of the day the bad outweighed the good and I just couldn't allow myself to go on like that. He's had many different affairs with a variety of girls the one that hurt the most, was the one that continued for almost 3 years. I fooled myself into believing that I could still make it work because I loved him with all that I am. But then reality hit and I realized it could never work until I healed from all the pain. I don't feel good enough for anyone. Things went so far that he almost physically abused me once. I still love him very much and hope that we can one day be together again. But I just can't be with him right now. He feels that I'm selfish and I'm such a selfless person. I was never going to break up with him, but I don't deserve to be this depressed. He calls me all sorts of names and thinks that I'm cheating but I didn't break up with him for someone else I did it for myself. To gain back my self-confidence and realize my worth. I don't know what to do because he still messages me every day and I don't have anything left to say to him. I feel bad, but I think about everything. 7 years too long and now the thought of him disgusts me. Am I being selfish to put myself first after 7 years? I mean I gave my relationship everything and now that he

feels he's done cheating I must just carry on and
pretend as if I was good enough all these years
knowing there's no trust, respect, or loyalty in
this relationship? I don't know what to do. I'm
becoming more and more depressed every single day of
my life. My schoolwork is getting effected, my
mental state is all I have.

Dear Anonymous

I want you to highlight "he almost became
physically abusive" and let that be your sign to
let go of everything. Anyone who puts their hands on
you, or tries, or even thinks of it, is a disgusting
person. A person who doesn't deserve the good that
was brought into their life. Some never see the good
because they never deserved it, and that's what you
need to understand. If something doesn't work out,
and nothing you do changes the vibe, that's another
sign, walk away. When you stick around where you're
not wanted, you'll just repeat the same hurt that
you're feeling. You can't fix what you didn't do,
you can't change someone's heart, if they love
you, they love you. But the love you feel may differ
from their kind of love, and that's when you need
to take a step back and see if the love, they're
reciprocating is healthy, or just to keep you
around. Toxicity makes company off vulnerably; it
lives when it can take advantage. I can't speak off
your heart, because we all loved when it wasn't the
right time, or the wrong person, but I just want to
share, if he really loved you, after all those
years, he would of never hurt you. Sometimes we stay
because we use love as an excuse, without taking in

the reality of the situation. Sometimes we're afraid to move on because we hold faith close to our hearts in hopes people change. Sometimes we're just in love with the idea of love and attach it to anyone who gives us an ounce of it. Your self-worth and the love you keep giving will always be empty until you let go of the blame, until you let go of the pain. Open your eyes.

Anonymous 36

I'm in a relationship and falling hard and fast. I still feel this little feeling that he's possibly talking to or entertaining other women. I'm scared to bring this up because I don't want to seem so insecure. I'm honestly very scared because my last relationship I was cheated on all the time and I don't know if I'm just so messed up, and I'm doing this to myself.

Dear Anonymous

I think insecurities are normal when it comes to years of dealing with toxic behavior. But I also believe you need to take time for your own to work out them too. I believe self-reflection is important, even if you weren't the one to inflict the toxicity, sometimes we're to blame too, for putting up with it. It's important to work it out, so when the next person comes along you won't inflict them with the same pain. Insecurities are dangerous, they can cause you to lose the one you love because of past events, that you think will repeat because there's no trust. Coming back to an understanding of trust and self-love is a journey, especially when you've gave someone all of you. But time is one thing to be true, don't let your insecurities ruin a good thing, but don't be blinded by love. If your intuition tells you otherwise, believe it.

Vent below:

_____

_____

_____

_____

_____

_____

_____

_____

_____

Scariest thing I've ever witnessed
was someone apologizing for their wrongs,
then repeating the same toxic behavior,
having no idea how cold they are.
It's scary when you want to love someone,
but they make it completely impossible.

Anonymous 37

I was in a relationship for a year and a half with a guy who was mentally abusive. I'm an extremely outgoing person and love life. He sucked all of that out of me. He wanted to get married and I was all on board for it. He would insult me and make me feel like half of myself. I'm a college basketball player and he was too. I won some amazing awards and every single one he would never tell met he was proud, but instead he would tell me I didn't deserve it and discredit me. He didn't even show up when I received an award while telling me I looked ugly when I did. I always came around his family and did everything I could with them because family is important to me and him. However, never did he ever come to any of my basketball games and go and sit and talk with my family. He would tell me how bad it was that my dad didn't approach him. He wanted me to stop talking to my dad and move to a different state with him. I was so blindly in love with him that I was so set on doing that if it meant being together. He never met any of my friends and told me he didn't like them. My second half is my gay cousin and he would say the worst things about him. I was always the first to be around his friends and I wanted to. I woke up every day for a year and a half ashamed of the life I lived outside of our relationship. I wasn't allowed to be myself. I had to stop doing everything I did to make him happy and I blindly did it. I don't even think my message can tell you how bad this truly was. I've been out for

less than two months and I have been finding myself,
forgiving myself and loving myself. I've grown
leaps and bounds but I have so much more growth to
do. I'm scared to love again because this love was
so blind and hurt me and took me out of everything I
am.

Dear Anonymous

I want to say how incredibly heartbreaking
this story is, I felt it. I'm very sorry for the
time you lost being caught up in someone else's
life you never took time for yourself or was able to
know who that was. It's terrifying, to love someone
but also feel like you lost everything else that
also means something to you. When someone is making
you choose between what you love, and them, always
choose what you love, even if they're a part of
that. Because truly, just because you love him
doesn't mean you need to keep him in your life. I
felt the toxicity grow stronger. I felt he loved to
control you. He is a very selfish person, and a very
selfless person at that. He isn't good for you, and
that's what I found written beneath your message. I
was once blinded because I "loved" someone, I
changed my whole life and decided to do things to
make them happy, and I have to say, looking back, I
wish I would of spoke up on things when they went
down, but I was too comfortable to walk away. I
hated change and I never wanted to hurt him, but he
was killing me slowly, the me I was before I met
him, the me I was afraid to be. The more I became
that person, the more we fought and the more we
disconnected. I learned the beginning of
relationships are always the times most cherished,

and if things start to fade, don't overlook the change. There were so many signs in the universe that spoke to me, but I was too deep in to look the other way. My best advice is to take every piece of this as a lesson in what love wasn't. The love you will build within yourself to be able to give to another, one day, will be like nothing you felt before. It's important to know that love doesn't hurt, to know how powerful love really is. I'm praying for you.

Anonymous 38

I've been dating a guy for over a year and 3 months he hasn't told his baby mother he's dating me. They've not been together for over 4 years. He says it's because his ex-wife kept his other kids from him when he was dating someone, and he never saw them and had to pay a lawyer to see them. He doesn't want to go through that again. I feel like it's a dead end when we talk about this.

Dear Anonymous

I've never been in a serious relationship or a relationship at all for that matter, with someone who had a child, and honestly never will be, so I can't give you a lot of advice on that. But I will add that keeping secrets from anyone will lead to nothing good, only hurt will be the ending. Because truly, coming from my view, there could be many different things going down, or lies being told. He could want his cake and eat it too. His baby mothers have no right to keep his child from him just because he's with someone else, unless there's

something else going on. It just doesn' t sound
right, neither does the fact he completely shuts it
down when you bring it up. My best advice is leave
while you can, if you have no prior attachments to
this person. You shouldn' t be with someone who
isn' t proud to love you.

What do you think?

_____

_____

_____

_____

_____

_____

_____

_____

_____

People will be fake with you for so long, but the
moment you let them go, they flip the story and make
you into the bad guy.
It' s how every toxic story end.
There are better people out there, ones that will
love you, not just love you for the moment.

Anonymous 39

A betrayed love due to a terminal disease.
The marriage is done, but my blood cancer was the
catalyst she used to end it. She said I made it up I
don' t have enough oncology visits to have cancer.
It' s painful because it' s so real.

Dear Anonymous

Unfortunately, I can' t provide advice,
because I honestly can' t even imagine, but I can
feel your pain. I want to say I' m very sorry you
had to be put through so much stress from someone
you loved, someone you were married to, vowed to
love through it all, but couldn' t get that same
reciprocated back to you, I' m sorry you had to go
through such heartache to realize she wasn' t the
one for you when it came down to forever. I pray
you' re in a better place without her, and your
health has improved. I pray you didn' t lose
yourself within all of this.

Anonymous 40

I was with someone for 5 years and we
recently broke up a year ago, and he now has a new
girlfriend. I' m not sure how long but during
January of this year he expressed to me how he felt.
I told him we' re doing this back and forth again and
it' s not giving us time to grow as an individual.

We unfollowed each other on all social media and now recently I've been receiving private phone calls, I didn't think it was him, but this one night he called on facetime on accident and I just never responded. Now, my heart has been heavy, and I've been thinking about reaching out to him, but I don't know if I should. Yes, he has a girlfriend and out of respect for his girlfriend, I don't want to spark anything or come between them, but my question to you is, do you think I should reach out to him?

Dear Anonymous

To be honest, I can't really speak on whether you should reach out, because I'm unaware of why you two broke it off. Speaking from a place of the unknown, I would say follow your heart, because our hearts always lead us in the right direction. If all signs pull you in the direction, don't overlook it. Follow your heart, even if hurts someone in the process, the universe won't keep giving you the same cards and expect you to deal from another deck. If it's presented to you, don't look the other way.

People will stay in relationships they outgrew and expect happiness to come from it. Well listen, nothing good will come from something that's no longer in the cards. The more you force, the more the relationship becomes toxic on both ends. One see's the other has already walked away emotionally, but decides to fight because they love them, and the other decides to hold onto them because they don't want to hurt them, but search for attention elsewhere. This ends in pain, which could be resolved with communication. A word of advice: if you're not happy, let your partner know, because they're aware, but are holding onto you because you're confusing them. The pain you bring upon them will overcome, but the longer you hold them close the more toxic the relationship becomes. I don't believe toxicity just comes in physical abuse. I believe the biggest toxicity comes from mistreating yourself which creates toxicity in the one you love or wish to set free. Always playing victim doesn't make you a good person, especially if you can't be accountable. You can't be scared to let someone go because you don't want to hurt them. You're hurting them more by holding on knowing you don't love them anymore.

I hope you always choose you,

if you' re ever faced with that decision.
I hope you always remember how important you are.

Never lose sight on being the most important person
in your life. There are times you'll forget who you
are and put the needs of others before you. You
can't take care of them, if you're not taking care
of you. You can't love to your full potential
without setting the foundation.

It's one thing,
to speak something into existence,
but to make it happen
is what's going to put it all into perspective.

We all once loved someone,
to the point it made no sense,
because the love we gave only made sense to us.
We loved someone
whom never reciprocated any part of that love,
but we wanted love to surface,
so, we accepted less than we deserved,
having no idea what that was.

The worst thing you could do,
is let someone make you believe the love you give
isn' t enough,
so, you keep giving more,
without knowing how consuming it is,
to give all of you,
for the need of someone
who doesn' t even see your worth,
  toxic people are dangerous.

You can' t fall in love when searching for it,
or chasing trying to make someone love you.
Falling in love is when someone walks into your life
unexpectedly, and makes you wonder
what kind of love you' ve been consuming,
because their love
is the love you' ve been needing all along.

The love your chasing,
is the love you see among others.
The love you wish to feel but won' t ever receive,
because love can only be felt.
The love you see, may come in disguise.
The love meant for you, won' t ever make you blind,
it will open your eyes, to all the times you were.

Note,

Just because you're born to love,
doesn't mean everyone is someone to love.
Just because you have a connection,
doesn't mean you are soulmates.
Just because you gave all you had
and didn't get it reciprocated
doesn't mean give up.
Love will find you when it's time.

Just because you brought me pain,
I don' t wish the same for you.
I don' t want the same karma coming for me
that' s coming for you.

I outgrew a lot of people
I prayed to keep close forever,
but I realized
God isn' t going to keep people close to me
just because of love.
I' ve trusted him,
to remove anyone from my life
that doesn' t fulfill the purpose
my soul needs to grow.

I'm at peace knowing
what wasn't meant for me,
wasn't going to kill me.
Who wasn't meant for me,
is doing just as well as me,
I once loved you,
as though the love wasn't forever,
every moment is a moment I will remember forever.

You'll always continue
the same patterns with spiteful people,
they swear they'll change
you'll end up questioning
why you thought it was possible
to keep trying to save them
when you know you don't have the strength
to keep giving your energy away,
and your heart, so easily.

People are afraid to let go
of toxic situations
because they hold onto
every good memory they have of someone,
and attach to it,
thinking the exact feeling will revisit again.
Toxic people are like drugs,
having you search for what's gone
destroying you slowly in the process.

If you can' t ever admit
to being wrong,
and holding toxic traits
from the past
letting them shape you,
how are you supposed to grow?

You can' t always blame others
for the way they treat you
when you' re the one allowing them to.

Maybe you' re the toxic one

Anonymous 41

I've been in a verbally abusive and controlling marriage for almost 10 years. We have two small children. For years I was in denial, very hurt by his words and behavior. I would seek help from our church and my daughters God parents, but they would only encourage us to get help together (he refused counseling) and doesn't believe in divorce so that was never an option coming from them. His words started to numb the pain to where I almost felt like I had no feeling left. Last summer I started doing more self-care, I hired a babysitter to help with the kids once a week so I could have more time to myself, I hired a housekeeper, and I started doing some real soul searching. I soon discovered that I indeed deserve so much more, and this life isn't it. He will never respect or appreciate me and will never change. I have hired a lawyer and am now reaching out to domestic abuse contacts in the hope that they can help me build up my strength and courage to move forward and get out. Right now, I feel depleted, weak and helpless and I just need some exercises and people to motivate me to stand tall, charge through and never look back. I'm scared.

If you wish to reflect:

_____

_____

_____

_____

_____

_____

_____

_____

_____

Anonymous 42

My most recent relationship has been over a
year now. Even though I can't say I'm over it.
Every day it seems to be on my mind since the
breakup. Her, the situation, words said, last
encounter and more. Why? I don't know. She was my
best friend. The last conversation aside from our
last encounter, she said she couldn't imagine a life
without me. How she still wanted to be friends. Of
course, at that time I couldn't even imagine doing
so. She just broke up with me. Even though we had
our ups and downs I thought we were better than
that. We have been on and off for almost 5 years.
Which has been my longest relationship, maybe that's
why it has been longing on my mind. The times we
have been on and off we somehow found our way to
each other. Maybe that's why this time around I
decided to never give in to her. In the sense where
I would always make the first move or fight the urge
to message her first. Last summer I was close to
messaging her because a close friend said that she
felt some type of way and wanted to be friends too.
But throughout our whole relationship I was always
the one chasing her and doing things for her to make
her feel comfortable. It would be easier for me to
conform to what she wanted. She was not fully out
the closest. Which was a huge obstacle over the past
few years we haven't got past that. It was
difficult but there would be no way that I could
take that away from someone until they are ready to

do so themselves. Our relationship was pretty much
hidden, and I think towards the end it was
influenced by a close friend. This is the same
friend who was twisted and instigated something so
hurtful that ensued in my last encounter with my ex.
Now that is a whole new trip. It was NYE and my so
called other "good friend" likes to blame alcohol
and other substances because she hit on my ex.
Honestly such a shame to ruin what we had. My ex and
I, got along very well, caught up on life. Then shit
hit the ceiling when my so called "friend" made
moves and my ex vice versa. Our best friend who
loves drama stirred up that situation, instigating
them two together. Knowing that my friend knows my
history. We talked every day and hung out every
week. How could she do that to me? And to blame it
on alcohol and substances? How? She is older than me
which makes me think, doesn't she know better? Three
people who were once so good to me in my circle,
made my life come crashing down yet again. I had to
pick myself up and get away. Had to use my days off
from work to leave the city to re-cooperate and see
my other best friend. I'm so glad I did, had a
moment to get away and be surrounded by good vibes
only. Last thing I ever said to my ex was when I had
found out that her dog died. Knowing this, I know
that her dog meant a lot to not only herself but to
her family. So, I sent the house flowers. Didn't
think I would get a response, but I did. Which was
nice. Every time I look at every encounter, I had
with my ex. The outcome is always be being the
better or bigger person. I always question why I do
this and that. When others tell me that I don't have
too or shouldn't do this and that. As much as I want
to be upset or sad or whatever, is it because I

still care? Probably but at times it makes me miss our friendship of course. I can't change people and they won't change either. Maybe her ego is so big, as far as I have known her. Her pattern with people that she has lost is such a shame. Because I have become one of those in her past because she can't own up to certain things or doesn't want to be the first to message. Sometimes I wonder how she could let me; a good thing go I gave her everything, time and space and infinite love. She is right though when she said that I deserve better. And deep down I know I deserved better because I wasn't getting the same love reciprocated. All in all, this has been one of the hardest things I've ever had to do and overcome. Life has been a trip since, but I've grown so much. I've been doing so well. Knowing what I need to do for myself to be a better person and to heal. Surrounding myself with positive vibes only and with positive people. Life goes on and I had to grow. I've become a better version of myself, when I thought I would never get over it. I'm proud of myself when I look back at how far I've gotten and of course I know that I have always been true to myself. It is exhausting even thinking about all these things but writing this all out makes me feel so much better.

If you'd like to reflect:

_____

_____

_____

Anonymous 43

I'm a 41-year old mother, of 3 amazing
children and 1 grandchild. My life has been full of
so much loss. I lost my sister who I was very close
to when I was 13, my father a few years later and my
mother about 3 years ago, basically I have no family
left. These last two years have been the hardest due
to the ending of my 23-year relationship with my
husband/high school sweetheart, due to his
infidelity. This caused such a tidal wave of changes
it was unbelievable! I decided to end my 12-year
career with the company I worked for, I sold all my
belongings, I moved from the west coast to the east
coast, leaving the only place I've ever known as
well as my friends. It's been such a journey, I've

been discovering myself, finding the self I lost somewhere in all the chaos that was my life. With nothing but my faith and my writing to turn too. I love your writing because it gives words to some things that we sometimes can' t find for ourselves. If there' s anything, I' d love to see you write, it would be the road we have before us is not easy. I' m still experiencing disappointment and heartbreak. But I have faith all things happen for a reason and that no matter what when I look back, days, months or even years from now I will see how far I' ve come, I won' t recognize who I left behind. It' s so hard sometimes to take that higher road and not treat the ones who are doing me dirty the same as they do me, but I know in this world you get what you put into it. It' s hard at times to tread on with no parent or my best friend, my sister to turn too, but I pick up a pen and write. I know death, disappointment, and heartbreak is not done with me. But I also know that neither is the joy, the love and blessings we experience. We easily get lost in the darkness. I' m not the woman I was three years ago, sometimes it was a few well written words that kept me going. Thanks for those.

Dear Anonymous

I love how you made this story end so beautifully, and how you had the strength to just leave and not look back. I' m very sorry for all your loss. Death is one of the hardest life lessons to understand, forget over-come, because it' s impossible to completely overcome death. It comes, for everyone, especially ones we love, at times we

don't expect, and some we do, but neither are easy.
It hurts to lose someone so close to your heart,
even a stranger it hurts to see death upon someone
who wasn't a loss to us, but to someone else, it
still hurts. I had my fair share of "losses", but
I have given death a different perspective, I no
longer like the term "sorry for your loss" because
I didn't completely lose them, only in physical
form, but in spirit they're still alive. I have
come to terms with death of a very close loved one
of mine and it took a year of panic attacks, crying,
being lost, deep depression, and isolation. Today,
I'm at a place in my life where I've saw the
beauty in the spirit that lives on, that guides me
every day, and instead of being sad, I choose to
love what God still blesses me with, a beautiful
guardian angel. Sometimes it's harder to cope when
I really sit and think, but I try to not let myself
fall into that dark place again. I like to remember
her as she was, as she still lives within me, near
me, every day. I live how I know she would want me
too, because no one that passes every leaves, and
that's what's gotten me through. The road before
us isn't easy, especially when it comes to trying
to cope from things that seem far out of reach, but
to always remember every day is another day to live.
Don't worry too much about yesterday because it's
gone, don't spend too much time on what comes next,
because things change in minutes. Focus on where you
are now, in the moment, because that moment could be
your very last, or could turn into the rest of your
life. Live every moment like it's your last.

What are your thoughts about death?
Does it scare you?

_____

_____

_____

_____

_____

_____ is my biggest fear.

Why?

_____

_____

_____

_____

_____

_____

5 ways to overcome it:

1.

2.

3.

4.

5.

Anonymous 44

Two months ago, I met a guy on a dating app. From the second time we met, he touched my hand already. He became very touchy afterwards. He was so nice, and he picked me up with his car. He was paid for all the meals we went to bar and had some wine. He was able to take care of me. I thought he was kind and mature enough. Until one day, he made a comment about my appearance. Such as, "I think you should try to smoothing your hair, it will look better on you, I think you should make an appointment and take care of your acne, I think you should start to lose some weight." At that time, I was blinded by his love and his kindness. And every time he made a comment about myself, I would say sure, I will. I was too afraid to stand up for myself. Even when I was talking to him, I was being way too careful. He was sensitive, and I did respect that. Until one day, I made one tiny mistake, I forgot that we made a deal not to talk about our past, but I was accidently talk about it. He was pissed, and disappointed. He said "you're such a deal breaker" then he made comment about my flaws, was heartbreaking. Then decided he doesn't want to deal with me anymore. He doesn't care about me, and he wanted to move on. And open his heart for the new opportunity with new girl. My self-esteem was running low. And I felt worthless. It seems like, I wasn't good enough for him. I was stupid for making a mistake and hurt his feelings. Until one day, I met his best friend. And his best friend said "he may be insecure about himself. He doesn't wanna know about your past, because he was afraid" I don't have time to deal with guy and his insecurities. Ever since, I'm blessed. I knew his true colors. He would talk about my appearance, so he could feel better about himself. He was mentioning my flaws, and make it seems like he couldn't handle me, not anymore. Because I was too much for him, and there's no room for mistakes, and I knew that he would want to be with the perfect girl. It hurts, knowing there's a guy, who sees me as an asset. Or investment. Instead of being kind, honest, and true to me. We had sex multiple times. I feel that he was using me. Took advantage of my body and my heart, meanwhile he was not 100% sure with his feeling towards me. I was heartbroken. He made me feel small. He was 5 years older than me. I was 21 years old. And he broke my heart into pieces. He made me feel like unwanted. My love for him was pure. And I did care about him, a lot. He was fake, and he was branding himself all the time. He was insecure that I might leave him after knowing who he really was. He was afraid, the thought of me, being capable of loving him. His kindness wasn't real. I shouldn't believe in him. It's okay. God will take care of my heart.

Dear Anonymous

_____

_____

_____

_____

_____

_____

_____

_____

_____

_____

Anonymous 45

I'm finally letting go of the love of my
life. In the grand scheme of things, it's no big
deal. People move on, some had it worst. But you
see, I deserve this. I never really understood how
people's lives crumble when they undergo a breakup,
love is love, it isn't so bad one moves on, until I
met you. every time I get to spend more time with
you and the more I get to know you, the more I get
scared, because I keep on falling for you each time
but the nagging part is we do not have a future
together, because you belong to someone else. I was
stubborn and selfish and went along my unbridled
emotions. Despite that, I honestly and secretly hope
we shall be together, not now but in the distant
future. With you it's easy to bear my soul. I'm a

whole new other woman whenever I'm with you, I discovered I have courage and strength I didn't expect I possess. I like the me when I'm with you. I'm the best version of myself when I was with you. I shared my struggles and the things that matter and what you say means a lot. It's you I draw my strength from. I keep on asking myself, how am I ever going to pick up the pieces? You said this is worth fighting for and I trust that with all my being. But you left me. The pain I'm feeling over losing you is way more than I'd like to admit. I keep on telling myself it's going to be okay and yet I can't even dare being with someone even in fantasies because just like him, they will fail and leave me as well. When I think of what was, it still makes me feel giddy inside and I'd still catch myself smiling. Perhaps, is focus on the happy times and not those times he made me feel bad or sad. When logic sets in, devoid of any feelings the fact is, he wasn't strong enough to choose me then, he certainly isn't now. Sometimes I tell myself I deserved to be treated like a rug, left in limbo. Your worth isn't diminished by how some people value you. Be purposeful not boastful. Value your worth and work but set aside your pride. Love I felt is not real love because people got hurt along the way, it was selfish, and most of all I was unkind to myself. I let myself believe that our past was not done but what I failed to see is that, he was part of my past for a good reason. There's no sense digging that up. What's meant to be will easily find its way to me.

Dear Anonymous

Vent Below:

Anonymous 46

He was the first person I ever loved. He made me love him, then left to be with someone he loved. At first, I understood, but slowly it turned into hatred and rage. Because it felt like he took everything from me. My self-love, my mental health, which was in amazing state. My virginity. Everything. Throughout the time we were together, he was also with her. I was his little secret, and it didn't matter to be because I loved him. When she eventually found out, I was carrying his child. But it didn't matter. He still left. He put me through so much stress that I lost my child, and when I told him, he didn't even care. He never spoke about it, he didn't cry, nothing. I was in my worst state of mind. Every day was another day of hell. My grades and attendance got worse, I wanted to drop out. I wished I wasn't alive, with my child. I think that was the worst of all of it. Your first child is supposed to be the best thing ever, mine didn't even make it. I've recovered a lot. But all that happened within seven months. It was the worst, and slowly I'm getting better, but I see him every day and it haunts me. Knowing he doesn't care and never will. Knowing he's still with her. I'd never wish such pain on anyone. It feels good to get it out, since it's something I don't talk about often. But people need to know that no matter what you do for someone, they'll always be in it for themselves.

Anonymous 47

About 6 years ago around this same time, I
was taken to a local hospital for a 5150 hold for
attempting to commit suicide. I had just ended a 4-
year relationship with an ex-boyfriend. Throughout
that relationship, I completely lost myself. I lost
interest in school, I had a shitty relationship with
my family, I lost almost all my friends, and even
though in my eyes it seemed to be okay since I had
my significant other, my life was just getting worse
and worse by the day without even realizing it. Just
like any other relationship. The first 2 years were
magical. I thought he was my soulmate and we would
be together till the end. But suddenly, I started
feeling a hole in my heart, like something was
missing. Like something inside me was yearning for
something more. I started feeling like this was
because of the abuse I experienced. A small fight
would turn into a never-ending war. I got shoved,
spit on, told the most disgusting things you can
ever tell a human being, and yet I continued to
stick around in hoping that one day this person
would change or show me the love I felt I deserved.
That time never came. At this point, I had already
been unfaithful to him since I thought those other
loves would fill me with whatever he couldn't. There
were days I would run away and just sit on a bench
and dial the suicide hotline because my heart and
soul just couldn't take it no more and I didn't
know where to go or who to run to. He stripped

almost every part of me, and I felt like a ghost who didn't accept that it had died. Towards the end of it all, I had found someone who wanted to show me what love was about. Someone who was ready to take me in and help me heal my wounds since he too experienced the abuse right in front of his face. They always say that you should let your heart heal in order to prepare yourself for a greater love but with him, I just wanted to dive into that love immediately. That was when I decided to close that chapter of my book and never look back. Today I'm happy to say that my heart is so happy to be with my true soulmate and to be with someone who not only loves me with every ounce of him, but also loves himself in order to be able to give me this eternal and unconditional love to me.

Dear Anonymous

It's beautiful, to be able to feel your happiness, and love, so deeply and we don't even know each other. But through your words, I felt that. Being an empath takes a lot from you but gives you the best ride of your life. Us empaths, we love wholeheartedly, we love when it's not love-we love unconditional. Loving unconditionally could confuse some when it comes to being hurt because of how big your heart is. Love isn't painful, love isn't a constant force. Love is a feeling that can't be denied, only some lie. Love is made out to be dark, because so many chose bad choices of words when they feel a connection, or find someone who does good by them, who loves them unconditionally, but isn't up to reciprocate it to you, or anyone for that matter. Some aren't ready to love you, or may never, but

don't let that get lost in them. When you love
someone, you love them for their heart, mind, and
soul. Some may say cliché, to love yourself first
before you let anyone in. I live by this, because if
you give all of you because you know your hearts
big, and the love you have, to give is untouchable,
you'll get lost within them everytime. The worst
thing you could do, is get lost in someone you love,
to the point you no longer recognize yourself.
Losing yourself, looking in the mirror and not
connecting with the self you see looking back.
Don't ever give up things you love, people you
love, away, at the cost of someone else, if it's
not in your best interest. If this is forced upon
you, that person doesn't love you. It's the
scariest thing, to love someone so much, you
literally give them all of you, to the point you no
longer see you. Some of us wasted years of chasing,
some of us didn't make it. Some of us are still
healing. Some of us are still searching. Some of us
are still learning. But throughout this, we never
stopped loving.

Dear Anonymous

Come back to this page every day to write a
positive reminder.

Anonymous 48

My entire life I've been abused. As a child I was abused sexually, physically, and mentally by my father. My mother was verbally abusive, and I never received the love and nurture that I needed. Into adulthood I sought that love I never received as a child from men who were toxic and abusive in different ways. I just left an abusive relationship and still have nightmares about it as well as anxiety attacks. Through the years I've also suffered with depression, substance abuse, and suicide. I'm am struggling to love myself and be kind to myself. I am struggling to find peace and I am my worst critic. Overall, I just wish to be happy and healthy while learning that it's ok to be alone and that simply because someone doesn't love me doesn't mean I'm unworthy.

Dear Anonymous

My heart hurts, because you never deserved to be treated like you aren't good enough, as if you're not worthy. Some people are just not good people, and there's not much more to the story than that. Some people like to break you down to give themselves power. They don't have "power" they just end up having control over someone vulnerable, which indeed is wrong. A lot of our mental health issues come from the stress, and the surroundings we adapt to. All the love we attach to the wrong people, all the love we use as an excuse to make something wrong, right. Finding peace within yourself is a tough road, you hit a few bumps, some dead ends, and roadblocks, but nothing is impossible. You need to remember no one is you, no one has the power you do, when it comes to you. Your mental health doesn't make you a difficult person, it just makes you a different person, and different isn't something to be ashamed of. We all fight our own demons, some of us take longer to see the light after being lost in the darkness. Don't let anyone make you feel you're not worth of loving, of being true to you. Don't let anyone make you feel you're not worthy because you have the biggest heart some may never understand, because some may never be ready for it.

Anonymous 49

I guess you can say I've moved on but never got closure. Every now and then I ask myself what I did wrong and I get scared to let myself be vulnerable again in any relationship. I was fresh out of high school and I moved in with my boyfriend and his mom, he was sweet, but over time he started changing and one of my friends started messaging him behind my back. I guess she wasn't happy with her relationship. Well we were a month shy of being a year and he was my first official love, after all, I lost my virginity to him. He broke up with me and I later found out couple days later he got with my friend. They broke up because she cheated. But they ended up together anyways and got married. A year passed and I met someone new, we started as friends

and later became something more. For 2 years we were
on and off and I kept telling myself if I was
patient it would work out, he never let me post
pictures of us and couldn't tag him in anything. But
I didn't think nothing of it. He broke up with me
because he said he didn't feel the same and I guess
I can't blame him because I know people change. Not
even a week later on Facebook he became relationship
official with this girl and it hurt to see him move
on so fast that I questioned if he cheated and as
much as he kept denying it, my friends found a post
that proved otherwise. I felt broken all over again
like my first love but not as bad. Fast forward a
couple months I started talking to a friend and I
didn't think we'd end up together because we tried
and it didn' t work (trust issues on both sides) but
we found our way back to each other and my ex had
found out and he started calling me off and on
making small talk and bad talking the girl he left
me for, then later said they worked it out and I
told him I couldn't talk to him because it was
hurting and eventually I blocked him for my own
peace of mind. Fast forward now almost a year
throughout my new relationship, I got to a point
where I loved myself more than being hurt again. I
still question why I was never enough for my exes. I
question when my boyfriend speaks of the future of
us? It sucks putting up a wall and keeping it up
never allowing it to come down. Scared that any
moment I can be hurt the same way again.

Dear Anonymous

The first line that really stuck out to me, was "I never got any closure" that's where we always go wrong. When it's time to let someone free, we attached closure, trying to make sense of something that never had a reason. It's very confusing, loving someone who doesn't seem to give any piece of that love in return. It's more frustrating, to keep loving when we know there's nothing good coming to us. We fight to keep loving when we should be setting free. What I'm really trying to say, is we don't ever need closure. We convince ourselves we do, to hold onto what's already checked out. As you speak of the constant chase for his love, his wholeness, you always overlook the love he found in everyone but you, and when you found it, you put the blame on you. But it's no one's fault. He wasn't yours, anymore, or ever was how you thought. People grow. People change. We need to adapt. We need to accept, not everyone will love us for as long as we will love them. We need to teach less self-destruction, and more self-love. We need to stop giving ourselves so easily away to people with hearts that don't match ours, that aren't meant to fit. We need to stop chasing. We need to stop trying to fill a void that can only be discovered within. We need to learn, just because someone hurt us, shame on them, but when we become aware, and let them continue, it's shame on us. We need to take our blame too. We need to stop being afraid to keep loving, because we're too afraid to be hurt, again. We're stronger than we believe, our hearts, were meant to bleed. We were made to love, don't be ashamed to getting burned, but don't burn another because you're scared, you survived the heartache you didn't create, so don't create any.

Anonymous 50

On September 15, 2018 I was raped by a good friend of mine. I just got home from a wedding that night and I had been drinking with my family, when I got home I didn't want my night to end so I texted my best friend and asked her to hang out with me and she told me to go hangout with this boy, and if I do she would meet me there. Of course, I agreed because __ and I were kind of close, but not really. So, I texted him and he came and picked me up. I would say I'm tipsy but not drunk until the point where I don't remember anything. When we got to his house the first thing, he asked me was if I wanted to have any more to drink, and of course I declined because I didn't want to drink more. But he kept asking me repeatedly. So, I gave in and had some, but I didn't make the drink so I'm not sure what he put in it. I drank it and we talked for a little bit. Then we go up to his room and we are sitting on his bed, but we aren't super close to one another. We decided to watch a movie until the rest of my friends came. When I got the text that my friends were there that's when it truly hit me. Things started to get extremely blurry, and I have been drunk a few times before this incident, so I know my limit and I know I didn't drink that much so it was strange. But then this is where things go black. All I remember after that is waking up at my house in the morning. I went to the bathroom in the morning and I peed and when I wiped there was blood and I was sore, and I have never had sex before. My heart absolutely dropped to my stomach because I don't remember anything, so I texted him and he refused to tell me anything. I didn't tell anyone for a month. Until one day I got a message and it was this girl who had a screenshot of __ saying all that he did to me and how he knew that I wasn't aware. I was absolutely torn apart and I was scared because he is a popular boy and I was scared no one would believe me. So, I told my mother and she went with me to report it. I reported it and he admitted to the police what he did. When the police officer came and told me all he said to me was "At least it was only five seconds, could've been worse" which still makes me sick. So, I waited to see if he would be prosecuted. They didn't even contact me for a month until I finally called them. When I called them, they said the DA won't pick up the case and basically, he will get nothing for what he has done to me. I can't even get a restraining order against him because the school I go to would still allow him to go there even with that. I have tried everything to make my voice heard but I feel so silent. I'm not sure if you are going to read all of this but if you were to write about this, I would feel like I finally am being heard and would have some closure for what has happened to me.

Dear Anonymous

Some people are heartless, which have no understanding of the human heart, it's like they don't have one. I'm deeply sorry for that traumatic experience you had to go through, and not remember anything but to always wonder what happened. I'm sorry you thought it was a good friend of yours, how we are close to the same people who are so quick to hurt us. I'm sorry you need to live with the unsettling memories. I'm praying for you, and your journey to finding peace. Don't chase closure, because you won't find it. Closure is what we convince ourselves we need to move on, but we don't, instead, we need peace. You need to remember none of this is your fault, because you chose to trust a close friend, who chose to lie about taking what he wanted knowing you couldn't speak for yourself, at that moment. The more you chase closure, the more you'll come up short. Find peace, find the love in yourself. It's going to be a long road, don't get discouraged. Be patient. Stay true to yourself. Don't look back.

Anonymous 51

I broke up with my girlfriend a year and a half ago, blaming everything on her, only to now realize my own toxicity contributed to us ending and that I'm not the only one who left the relationship hurt. I looked at the entire thing selfishly and now our communication is too damaged for me to even apologize. I don't really know how to explain. Anything. But I guess I need closure when it comes to love and loss. This happened when I was in high school. My parents are the stereotypical Hispanic religious type of parents. Who are rigid and homophobic, I got help from a friend that was able to tell I was struggling to define my sexuality and helped me come out as bisexual, I understood what I was feeling for a friend was more than just friendship, it was love. I never acted on it because of my parent's disapproval of the LGBTQ community. I was too scared to act on my feelings in fear of being kicked out or hated by them. So, I started separated myself all together from her. Soon after both my friends got together. 2 years later I had started slowly reconnecting with her. But it wasn't enough. That same year she overdosed and passed away because she was in a new abusive relationship which I couldn't see or help with because of the distance I decided to create. I feel like I could have done more. She deserved more. As a friend and as someone I claimed to love.

Dear Anonymous

First things first, you never blame yourself for something you had no control over. I know you may have thought you would be able to save her, considering your history of love, but sometimes love isn't enough. And sometimes, people battle demons we can't cure, because it's not our demons to battle. People choose the life they decide to live, and she got herself into a life she wasn't prepared

for. I'm not saying she deserved everything that
has happened to her, because a lot of people become
blinded by what they believe love is, so it makes it
harder to overcome the toxicity. Toxicity truly
kills, and it's very scary to know someone can be
capable of making someone so broken. But at the end,
only the person within that toxicity can see the
light, only they can save themselves. It's not your
fault she chose a road which she couldn't come back
from, it's not your fault. Repeat that as many
times you need to, because I promise she wouldn't
want you to blame yourself. You two had something,
you loved and lost that love, there's no reasoning
other than sometimes love outgrows and we need to
move forward onto the next part of our life. She was
a piece of your story, but she's not your story.
You are your story. When it comes to love lost
there's no closure, there's only peace. Finding
peace in what once was, remembering the good,
forgiving yourself for the bad, and allowing
yourself to move on. Death is one of the hardest
things to come to terms with, and to move on from,
because this person you love is no longer in human
form and it's something all of us will never
completely understand. It's something we beat
ourselves up about because we can't balance loss
and love. We can't accept someone's road ended and
we're supposed to keep going. It hurts. It hurts so
badly to love again, because you feel you're
hurting them. But listen, when that someone loved
you as much as you loved them, you will see their
spirit live on. You will feel the love every day,
with little reminders you're not alone. But first,
you will live in pain searching for the answer,
until you realize there's no answer. Life doesn't

make sense, and it's not up to us to analyze it. Promise me you won't try to understand, and spend more time living.

Anonymous 52

I was in an abusive relationship from ages 19-21 and before I figured out who he really was, I was already living 4 states away from home. I lost who I was completely throughout the emotional, mental, verbal, and physical abuse. When I was finally able to get out of that situation, I entered the darkest period of my life. I truly don't remember the first 3 years of being back home. I had bottled up everything from that relationship and didn't tell anyone about the abuse until 4 years after being home. I've seen multiple therapists over the years, and nobody has ever understood me as much as my current psychotherapist. I'm currently 30 years old and I suffer from generalized anxiety disorder, social anxiety and panic attacks. I've also dealt with depression for as long as I can remember. But I can truly feel who I'm meant to be awakening inside of me. I'm finally learning to let go of things that have been subconsciously holding me back for years now. I feel inspired to write again after so many years of feeling stuck. I'm finding the will to continue with my life. It's a great feeling! I'm still holding out hope that the stigma on mental illnesses disappears. Just because you can't see the hurt, doesn't mean it's not there.

Dear Anonymous

I remember the first time I got my heart
impaired I lost complete control over the situation.
I became a fool when it came to them, and the
constant reminder that "I loved" them. I would use
the excuse of love to justify why I stayed. I tried
convincing myself they were real and loved me the
same. But when the ending hit, I was fool. I
remember years later, his girlfriend called my phone
because he told her he was going to be with me,
funniest part, we haven't spoken in a year, I cut
all ties when he decided to play me as the fool and
use my love as his own weapon. I wasn't physically,
mentally, but emotionally abused. I was manipulated,
used, and treated less than I deserved. I was young,
dumb, and vulnerable. A year later when his
girlfriend called me, she told me the whole time we
were together, he was also with her. I didn't feel
a thing. I wasn't hurt or mad, I felt bad for her
mostly, because she chose to be with someone who
could treat her so terribly. I was so damaged
chasing his love for years, I spend most of my life
after high school trying to make him love me. I
remember one night so vivid, when he poured out so
much hatred towards me because I caught him out on
everything, after that, it took me some time to
realize I wasn't wrong, and all the time I spent
loving someone who played me like a game. We get
lost in love and it takes up so much space in our

hearts, it makes it feel impossible to let go, or to feel something real, because now we never think we will feel. I know I can't put myself in your shoes when it comes to the damage he's done, the abusive he brought, but I can understand the pain you're now holding in because of someone who made you feel you're worthless.

Anonymous 53

I met him three years ago, and we were everything you see in the movies. The kissing on the beach, the sleepovers in his jeep, and laying on the roof staring at the stars, we did it all. But after 2 years of living together the spark faded, and I always tried to re spark it but like every relationship it must come from two sides. And soon enough I caught him flirting with someone else, adding people on social media, and liking pretty women's pictures, I felt like I put all my love, energy, and tears into the relationship. I don't think anyone knows how in love I was with him, he made my knees go weak, and in my eyes, he put the stars in the sky. But after forgiving him many times, it was as if that love faded to a point where I couldn't forgive anymore, and I left. After a while I met someone else, the feeling I get with him is far from what I felt for my last, but we get along extremely well. After getting to know him, I started to really like him, but I couldn't let myself get to close because I just felt like my heart still belonged to my last. I wanted to stay friends with him because I couldn't bear to think of a life without him, he was no matter what still the person that knew me best, and that I cared for

with all my heart. We went for rides often and after
a couple times, I noticed he started dressing up for
me, putting on my favorite cologne, and got out of
his Jeep every time we went for a ride just to open
the door for me. He told me he realized what he
lost, and I told him about the one I was seeing now
and I cried because I did miss him, I just kept
asking him "why did it not hurt you to see me cry"
"why did you do the things you did" and he said
that he didn't see what I had in front of him
anymore and he apologized to me. I told him we would
try to make it work again. He bought me flowers, but
the moment he wanted to give them to me, Clay came
walking out from the school and ended up not giving
them to me in front of him because he didn't want
Clay to feel hurt, and that just tells me so much
about him as a person. He told me that anyone would
be lucky to have me, and that he understood that
Clay liked me after getting to know me and that he
couldn't blame him. We are taking it slow, but
every time I see Clay (I told him me and Nickolas
were trying to work things out) he gets sad. He told
me he missed me and that he never felt a spark like
that with anyone. And I didn't know what to say, it
broke my heart to see him and not being able to do
anything about it. I don't know what to do. Do I
work things out with someone who I was head over
heels in love with, but after did the things he did?
Should we work things out and try to get to spark
back? Or should I choose someone I would want to get
to know better? I don't know what to do.

Dear Anonymous

Since you're asking me, I'll tell you from my honest view, anyone who entertains someone who's not you, doesn't deserve you. When you're in a relationship with someone you are the focus, they shouldn't be flirting with anyone else. You should have their attention completely. I was once with someone and I remember it was in the beginning of our relationship I looked through his phone (which I'm not proud) because well, insecurities 101: Don't look through your partners phone! But again, I saw him texting a girl which he received nude pictures from. She told him how pretty I was, he replied "she's okay, she looks better in pictures" I lost of my self-confidence, whatever I had left, of course. I was embarrassed to be with someone who thought so low of me, but I didn't bring it up to him because I chose to look through his phone, and wanted to continue, so I didn't speak on it. Some time passed and I went on our laptop, his Facebook was open, and I looked. I saw him talking to his ex before me, whom I disliked for many reasons, mainly because when we first started talking, he left me to go back to her. I was insecure when it came to her, and every other woman he entertained that wasn't me. The conversation was flirty. I chose to bring it up, instead of apologizing or acknowledging it, he deleted the convo and changed his password and told me to "stop looking through his stuff" that's also when I brought up the other comment I saw, which he denied until late last year and admitted he said, but said he lied to her. Apologizing three years later about something that broke me down and made me so insecure, we never saw eye to eye on this matter, I was always wrong, he was never. I stayed, we lasted almost 4 years until I chose myself. So, to answer your question, I would choose the road that doesn't need to be revived. I would choose the road that led me to happiness, not betrayal. I don't believe in walking away and coming back together if pain was the reasoning. Love will never be the same, you'll always be wondering if you're the only one, and you don't deserve to feel that.

Anonymous 54

I'm 23. This is my childhood. Things have been dealt with, and we still deal with some of the outcomes that our childhood brought. But we are fighting them. I was five, my dad was a short-tempered man with a small drinking problem, and my mom was taking care of four children and trying to keep the house clean, but the computer screen got her attention. She would meet men at night when my father was attending to his old aunt, a state away. Men, she would tell me that were my real father. My sisters had different fathers too, but these were lies. A person who couldn't stop lying. A person who created me in the womb, told me nothing but lies to make me happy. But the computer screen still made her happy. Poker and games that cost money we didn't have. Mom took care of the bills, and dad worked. But one night, bills were not being made. They would always argue, by the age of five, the screams were just common. I played with the barbies to stay quiet. Things got too rough one night, my dad hit her. Hit her enough to want to run away. Take us kids, pack clothes in garbage bags, and leave when he left for work. A mistake he will regret for the rest of his life. A mistake he will apologize to this day. New place meant to be home. But wasn't filled like one. A man who shouldn't be around kids, and a new man to give my mom attention. DCFS became common visits at this new school. To a person, that I had to lie too. Say I was happy where I was. I liked being there. I love my mommy and I don't miss my daddy. I feel safe. She can't afford taking care of four children, a court visit will happen, full custody might happen. We go back to the farm, where we deal with the yelling. Alcohol is barely drinking now. They kiss in front of us, to prove they love each other. But she was still looking at the computer. Poker and online men get her attention. The office smelled of cigarettes. 13 years later, bills were not being paid at all. Mortgage not being paid. Eviction will happen. We will have to move. A place where my father's ancestors-built land, a place where all the stupid shit happened, but still my home. Dad found a new house, and mom left a note saying she wants a divorce. A man who really loved her. A man going into depression. Mom left for a new job, to a new man. A man who made her stop lying. But she can still lie within a lie. A tongue that can twist so many things. A mom who isn't good for me. A mom I can't trust. She ended it with a message, after seven years, and he said he felt like he didn't

know her at all. She was the king of the chess game.
She could lie to move anyone in front of her.
Now with A whole new man, a man she said she wish
she had his kids with. A person who wished me out of
existence. A mom I don' t want. They say you can
divorce the people who are family. And I want to
divorce her. I wrote this poem myself. "There was a
time where she wasn' t a bad mom, I remember she' s
the one who made Teletubbies from icing on my
strudels"

Dear Anonymous

I' m deeply sorry, my whole heart to you,
that you had to go without the love of a parent
since you were just a child. A parent' s love is
important, especially when it comes to becoming the
person you grow into. But I also believe, the
lessons you were brought through either make or
break you, and from your story, I can feel your
strength. I grew up with both of my parents, dad
worked a lot, mom worked a lot. Both had multiple
jobs, my sister and I were well taken care of,
especially living with my Nana and Poppy, and all
the family who surrounded us. But once I entered
high school, my dad disappeared, he still lived in
the area, worked at the same job since before I was
born, my sister and I were still on his insurance,
but there was no word from him. We still faithfully
spent every holiday at my grandmother' s house (his
side of the family) I love them very much, and so
very thankful they stayed in our lives when he
walked out. He didn' t speak to them. He missed my
high school graduation, the moments which mattered

most to me, he missed all those moments. It wasn't until late 2017 when he came back into our lives as he found me on Facebook. It took a lot of time to come to terms with accepting the request, I wanted answers, I wanted to know why he became absent on us. I started to believe it was something with me, but I was young, and I don't remember the shift of everything going badly. I remember all the good times, how he went on all my school field trips, dinner dates, spilt custody. It didn't hurt when my parents chose to be a part, it hurt when my father decided to just disappear and act like we weren't important. Till this day, I don't know why he was absent, I won't ever get the answer I long for, but he's in my life now trying to make amends and make things right. It took some time to understand and accept having him in my life now won't make up for lost time, but I would only be hurting myself by not letting him be a part of my life.

Anonymous 55

I've always been the shy, introverted girl. I never said much in school and I've always been insecure. In my teenage years I was at my worst and I had a massive self-hatred and I talked so much down to myself. Started drinking, smoking, taking drugs, cutting. Anything self-destructive. I would sleep with boys even though I didn't want to but because I craved the acceptance and the feeling of being good enough for someone. I knew they only wanted my body and nothing more, but I still let them get it, and it made me feel like I wasn't worth more than that. I started believing it made me feel even worse than before, but I kept on doing it, for a very long time. I let them use me. I didn't believe I was worthy of love. I found out I had social anxiety when I turned 18 and I started treatment and it really helped me love myself and believe in myself more and I started being more independent. When I turned 19, I found out I also suffered from avoidant personality disorder and started treatment again and I'm still in treatment for it and I'm so grateful that I've started at a early age because I really developed a lot through the past year. It helped me get to where I am today and boosted my self-esteem and I've started to love myself more and gone on a self-love journey and I'm happier than I've ever been.

Dear Anonymous

I can attest to being, the shy introverted girl. I never spoke from being a child until late years of high school, well only to people I spent most of my time with, in classes or close friends I grew up with. I was very closed in for the most part, I didn't like speaking for projects, or to anyone, for that matter. A lot of people labeled me "the girl who didn't talk" which put a high risk of anxiety on me, which made me not want to speak at all. I had my few close friends who stuck around me, I barely changed my circle of friends, and it was rare when I made a new one. To this day I still cherish all the friendships, and acquaintances I made. I hold close the ones who never judged me and saw me for who I was. But the ones who always pointed out the obvious "you don't talk" never

heard a word from me, and if they see me on the
street don' t expect me to speak to you now. I have
social anxiety, but over the years it' s gotten
better. I had no love for myself, as I looked for
attention from others, too. I wanted to feel wanted.
To feel loved, but I never gave myself up. I never
let someone get that close to me. We look for love
within others who can' t fill that void because
it' s the love we need to give ourselves. Self-love
is one of the hardest destinations to find, we go
through many heartaches, and self-destruction to
realize our worth. I wish it was possible to love
our-selves easier than having to completely lose
yourself just to rebuild yourself. But all the
lessons, all the roadblocks, all the constant let
downs, they stand for your strength. The more you
learn, the more you love about yourself. It' s never
too late.

Anonymous 56

I met a guy in August on a vacation to
Greece. He' s from San Diego and I live in Denmark
(a small country in Europe) so there' s a lot of
distance. But I really like him. I' ve been visiting
him two times and we write and FaceTime every day.
But I' m just so scared. He' s everything I' ve ever
wanted. He appreciates me, he compliments me, and he
doesn' t only want me for my body. But I' m so
scared of him finding someone else or getting bored
of me. What if I' m just not enough or his love for
me isn' t strong enough to make us last. Because I
know mine is. I love this man and I see a future in
him and I' m willing to risk it all and move from my
country for him. I' ve getting so used to talking to

him every day that I just can't imagine not to, and it scares the hell out of me to think about waking up one day and he won't be there anymore, I really hope that day never comes. I'm just in a confused place in my life and I have no clue about my future or how it will unfold I'm just trying to enjoy the journey and trying to love myself as I am with all the good and the bad.

Dear Anonymous

I've been in two different long-distance relationships in my life and both were completely different than the other. The first one, was when I was 19. I finally started dating the guy I chased for years before, letting him fill me with his words and running with just that. He lived in New York, which was 2 hours away of me. He would take the bus (2-hour ride) for weeks to stay with me, I never spent time in New York, he only came to me. Our relationship was everything to me, because I finally got to be with him after chasing, and hoping, it was right in front of me. We spent our first moments together learning, each other more, because all the other times in the past he would come and go, and come back when he pleased, so we didn't know each other in person. We spent one day together which a good day, but all the rest were like picking up pieces that never meant to fit, but I always tried to make them. The distance became a problem when he spent less time with me, and more time in New York. I heard from him less, his phone was off most time, he influenced most of the conversation. When he was at my house he left most of the time to go party with his friends, coming back to my house around 5 a.m. high off Molly telling me how thankful he is to be with me, this was one of the moments I realized I was doing this all wrong. I was with someone who lied to me about their age, who never was faithful, who was my first, who I built all this "love" around, to realize he was a fraud. I was in love with the idea of love, and he was a lying, cheating, sucker who deserved the karma he got dealt. I didn't do long distance anymore. I was too insecure after knowing the whole time he had his in-house girlfriend back at home, as I was his runaway fool. Fast forward to last year, when I met my current partner, he lived in Florida so that made us 1,200 miles apart. We had an instant connection, one I couldn't deny, so I didn't. We dealt with a good 3 months of distance before he moved to be with me. I'm happier than I've ever been, and that time around I didn't have doubts like I did in the past. Insecurities are scary, they will eat you alive. My advice to you, is if you felt it to be true, don't overlook that feeling. But if you're having more doubts than happiness, I would look for the closest door, because you can't make something right that was never meant to.

Anonymous 57

I met this guy on social media in summer 2017 and we started texting each other and I really liked him. After I got to know him more and I came to the conclusion that he was perfect, he was a wrestler had a perfect body, blonde hair, the bluest eyes that you kind of drown in but love it at the same time, he was kind of bad and had his own car and a motorcycle. I was infatuated with everything about him. Pretty soon we decided we wanted to meet up and we found out we only lived 45 minutes away from each other. He drove all the way to come see me and take me on a date. We were supposed to see a horror movie (it) but I got us lost in the highway and we ended up being like 40 minutes late to the movie, so we just went to Wendy's and then to the arcade at the mall and had a good time. A month after that he officially asked me to be his girlfriend and I realized I was falling hard, fast. I now realize that it was mostly due to my emotional instability that I fell in love with him so fast (didn't grow up with my mom, dad was in prison, grandma who raised me died when I was 12) and I relied on him for too much. I relied on him for confidence, love, happiness. The more I loved him the more I began to lose myself, but I honestly didn't care because I had him, and he was all I could ever need. Because I was so overwhelmingly in love with him, I dismissed anything he did or said that would shatter my perfect image of him. He began to text less, and he would post things like I swear she's so perfect? but he never posted about me before so. One day in December we had only texted twice the whole day, then later that night he snapped me at 9:32 and I was so excited because I thought it would be a really cute selfie or something but it was him and this other girl lying in his bed and the caption read "yall bxtches back off" I was so shocked and hurt in that moment, all I can remember is going to my room and crying myself to sleep. The next day was Friday and I didn't go to school because I physically couldn't get out of bed or do anything. Then later that day I talked to him and asked, what was that? And he "said my friend", I was so angry because he thought I was that stupid or he wanted me to leave him. But I ignored it because I still wanted to be with him and would let him do me wrong 100 times over before I left him. Then a couple hours later I said were you being honest? He told me everything, in the end he chose her. The next morning (Saturday) I got up to go to work and I checked my phone to see if he had texted me, he did and I was so excited because I thought he had changed him mind and wanted me back but it was a picture of him and her kissing. They sent me home from work early that day because I wasn't functioning right, and I couldn't eat for 3 days then I started to force myself to eat because I knew it wasn't healthy to not eat. I decided maybe I wouldn't hurt so much if I convinced him to be my friend, that way I could still have him in my life. That only made things worse, on Christmas I decided I was never going to speak to him again, yet I still didn't block him on anything. Because I relied on him too much for my happiness I was completely lost, and I fell in a deep hole I wasn't sure I could get out of. It's like my life before him had no color but I didn't notice until he came and painted all these colors and made everything. Starting in January 2018, he would come back once a month and tell me how I'm beautiful and just talk to me and get my hopes up and stuff. It really held me back from moving on. Then in June he texted me and said he wanted to get back together because he should have chosen me, and he missed me and it wasn't until January of 2019 I had finally officially gotten over him, I didn't need him anymore, yet I STILL haven't blocked him. I think it's mostly

because I know he's lost and if he ever needs
someone to help him find his way or to just be there
for him, I wanna be there. I never want him to go
through anything alone or to have to struggle in
life so I can't leave him alone or stop talking to
him. But I know that if I ever want a relationship
with another guy I'm going to have to cut him off
because I know that if he's still in my life I will
never be able to put anyone above him or to put
anyone's needs above his. That day hasn't come yet
but I don't know what I'm going to do when it
comes. To this day we still talk, send nudes, do
general couple stuff even though he still has a
girlfriend but I'm kinda fine with it.

Dear Anonymous

I found myself in your story when you spoke
about overlooking what could ultimately end you
both. You overlooked the disrespect, the constant
signs you should of took the opposite direction. I
remember being so "in love" I took blame for pain
I didn't cause, pain that revived after the pain I
endured for the years of trying to be good enough,
to wanting to be loved. I pushed every wrong thing
to the side because I loved him. I discarded so many
wrongs, because of the blindness I formed, because I
loved him. I found myself in the parts you spoke of
playing the fool many times, while not understanding
why the pain always found its way. I once thought I
wasn't good enough because I wasn't ever first
choice, or spoke the truth too, and I blamed that on
my vulnerability, my need of wanting to be known for
my heart, as if the amount of love I gave made me

the winner. My love's not for everyone, some loved me more, some I suffocated, I never matched up with anyone when it came to soul connections, no one ever loved me the same, until this day. When I finally opened my eyes, I realized no one who loved me would choose me second, or make me an option, I would be the one, the only one, there wouldn't be an option. So, before you play victim, look what your allowing and then tell me how you don't understand.

Anonymous 58

It started when I was five. My father left, my mother cried, and we watched a Vhs tapes of Barney, over and over. That was the day I learned how to stop, rewind, and press play again on the VCR. All I remember was her crying and me not knowing why. They asked us where we wanted to go, I said that I wanted to stay, my younger siblings mimicked my answer and he left. The next year someone new lived with us. Sometimes he was nice but only when he drank a little, if he drank too much, he was cruel. As a biracial child my identity was something that never came easily. I was confused. Hearing the n word for the first time was confusing. Learning it was something said in hatred broke my heart. Throughout the years the verbal abuse was the least of my worries. We couldn't tell anyone what was going on out of fear we would be taking away. The first secret I kept. Even my closest friends didn't know the details of what a day in my life was like. I loved to sing. I loved to do well. I liked attention. We had a place to escape too but was felt up by a relative better than being threatened and called names. Secret #2. Years of verbal, emotional, and physical abuse caused me to be a mess. Stop living in the past some would say but I couldn' t let go of what hurt me. Thinking of walking to the pay phone in the middle of the night to call the police only to have my mother deny any incident when they arrived. Feeling his fist busting my nose when I deflected his punch. That was the first and only time my nose has bleed ever. Remembering her cries. All the late-night trips to nowhere just to get away. The reality was I feel in love with men who said I was pretty. I let them suck everything out of me. I did anything they desired sexually and physically. I have starved myself for approval. I have been beat and felt bad and cried to be taken back. I have cried because I wasn' t good enough. I have hurt. Wanted to disappear from the world until something happened. The right man gave me attention. The right man loved me. The right man keeps calm when I' m losing it all. When I cry because I remember what has happened to me, he reassures me that it will never happened again.

Dear Anonymous

_____

_____

_____

_____

_____

Anonymous 59

I was born into an abusive household, with three brothers, one older and two younger, even before I was born, I'd already disappoint my parents (they wanted me to be different, gender). I don't recall a lot of my childhood but my grandparents told me how my narcissistic mother scorned me specifically since I was very little, and even expressed how even as a tiny human I had a strong character and stood up for myself in whichever way I could, of course this meant going against my parents, as a "consequence" I would get hit every time I stood up. I was the social butterfly in pre-school but not sure when I became annoyed by everyone and distanced myself from my classmates and friends, always feeling left out but also not taking part in the fun. Come junior high I changed once again and regained some of my social traits from before, I had more friends but they were always criticized by my parents as well, I began to separate my life, giving my parents as little information as I could about what I cared and felt, making me ache because I didn't have someone to trust my deepest self with. As all this happened the house situation was worsening, by morning we would constantly be bombarded by shouting, sometimes even getting woke up by them accompanied by physical mistreatment, I remember one day I wasn't even awake and was lying face down on the bed, my mother barged in shouting and took me by the collar of the shirt and pulled up, making me wake up in shock since she was choking me with it. This happened at least once a week with anyone of us, and I had to learn to sometimes take the abuse just so I could go out with my friends one day and could vent out a little bit even though I had a burning desire deep in my soul to stand up and prove them wrong. The worst period of my life was going to high school. My campus only had up to junior high so we would have to move to another campus of the same school that had high school. At this point I was the only one in my family that loved the school and my friends there (my other brothers opted to move to other schools) but my parents didn't, so they forced me to go to another school that was far away and I didn't know anything about. This hurt me very deeply since I got to hear from my lifelong friends how cool the new school was and how much of a blast they were having while I was stuck in the other school. To add insult to injury my parents began to economically manipulate me, if I didn't do it, I wouldn't get this and so forth, to the point where I didn't even have clothes. This threw me into a depressed state, I didn't care about anything, my grades plummeted to the ground, I felt tired both physically and emotionally, a huge numbness all the time and had recurring suicidal thoughts every day, even getting to the point of having all set for the attempt, fortunately, I never came to actually do it, it didn't feel right to cause the same pain I was trying to avoid to people I loved and cared deeply about, the support from my friends was what kept me from crossing that line. I began to recover from the depression and became more aware about the abuse, I got to identify my mother is a narcissist, and my father and my brothers are her "flying monkeys" they not only enable but take part in the abuse. But I began reading up on narcissists and their tactics and finally all made perfect sense, all the gaslighting and mind games that created a thick fog suddenly dissipated, leaving me clear as to what they do and why. Of course, this didn't change how broken I feel sometimes, almost 20 years of constant put downs is something hard to overcome, especially if you're still on that same situation, and I noticed how broken and sad I felt. Sometimes I just become overwhelmed by this constant bombardment of agony and pain and feel like I don't know where I'm going or even what I want, just a heart broken wanderer trying to find some sense and love in this world.

Dear Anonymous

Anonymous 60

A few years back I had to move to a new city and start a new life. For me it was something very terrifying and I did not look forward to it at all. I just gotten out of the military and was recently divorced so my life was in flux. I had been to 32 countries, 33 if you count Canada, so I thought "how bad can this really be?" I had a career already in place, somewhere to live, a reliable vehicle, and a select few close friends to support me. I did the normal process of meeting coworkers and hanging out with them, attempting to date, engulfing myself in my hobbies, and making time to see family and friends on the weekends. Everything was going as well as could be expected, and then she happened.

Dear Anonymous

This woman popped up on my social media "people you
may know" and I found her attractive, so I friended
her. I made several attempts to talk to her but to
nothing. Then one day, she agreed to meet me for
some drinks at a local restaurant and I was very
excited. It was your typical first date and we went
our own ways, nothing extraordinary. Little did I
know she would change my life forever. A few days
later she came over to my place and my world changed
forever. This woman made me feel alive. She made me
feel safe. She made me feel special. She made me
HAPPY. We moved in together. We were inseparable. I
stopped caring about my job, even though I went to
work every day. I stopped talking to my close
friends, even though they supported me. I stopped
seeing my family, even though they loved me dearly.
This woman became my world and nothing else on the
face of the earth mattered. We laughed so hard at
the same things I knew for sure this woman was my
soulmate. She became my best friend and my greatest
desire all at once. It was mine. Then, after a few
years of complete and utter happiness my world
crashed around me. I came home from work on a
Tuesday, and she said, "I'm not happy anymore, I'm
going to stay with my mother for a while." I
remember it vividly. As if the knife is still in my
heart. Perhaps, just perhaps, we flew too close to
the sun. So, I spent the next week or so attempting
to get her to come home and I didn't receive much
response from her. She was all the sudden honest
with me and it turns out she was having an affair
and moved in with that man. Not her mother. To use
the word devastated is more than an understatement.
The earth and everything in it became meaningless to
me. Little did I know that this was the catalyst to

throw my mental health into chaos. I suddenly had to deal with things in my mind I had always pushed aside because I had nothing left. PTSD issues from the military (regret about things I was a part of) came forward with a vengeance. My mania and the need to be constantly busy was apparent. Then of course the depression was sure to follow the highs almost killed me a few times. My own mind exhausted me, but I could not rest. I wasn't eating. I wasn't sleeping. I wasn't forming complete thoughts. I wasn't being human at all. My mind was always awake, and I couldn't calm it. I decided to call my mother and she urged me to get some help. I got diagnosed with Bipolar. I was put on a light dose of Depakote and things felt good for the first time in a long time. Then, she came back into my life. The period between her leaving and sending me the "I miss you" text, and me finding out my mental health was all of 5 months. What did I do then? What any broken, lost, sane man would do. I let her move back in. Yes, the passion and friendship were stoked again to a blaze almost immediately, but so was the distrust. I also stopped seeking help and taking medication almost immediately because this woman was all I needed in life to survive. My mistake. Things never returned to where they once were and a few months later I asked her to move out. Only to find out she moved in immediately with the new person she had been talking to while we were together. Again. I could be described as severely bent, but not yet broken. I already had the foundation to help myself I just needed to. The family and friends I turned my back on accepted me with open arms because they loved me. I knew I had to put my mental health ahead of everything else and then I could move forward with

my life. I am bipolar. It's who I am and it's
nothing to be ashamed of. I have very high periods
where I'm invincible, and some low periods. These
changes can happen very frequently and quickly. But
it doesn't define me. It does not mean I'm broken.
It just means I'm highly susceptible to feeling a
lot. I am in fact human, but I can recognize things
in my head so much more clearly now and it's
wonderful. I am still taking Depakote. I have
healthy relationships with family and friends, and
life is quite good for me right now. I never want to
give her credit for helping me find myself, but she
did, unknowingly. All the hurt, crying, anger,
sleepless nights, wanting to not be alive, ignoring
family and friends, was all part of my life. Yet
here I am. Just a man with a heart looking for love.
I will find it, be honest with it, and it will be
the greatest thing ever.

How's your mental health?
Have you been taking care of you?

Anonymous 60

I'm 15 years old suffering from social anxiety. I tried opening this up to my parents, but they never understand me, so I stopped bothering about it. I hate myself for having this because, I wanted to like all the other teens who have full confidence of themselves and make friends, but as much as I want to try, the anxiety keeps eating me up. Sometimes people think everyone has a little social anxiety, but I completely disagree. Not everyone is afraid of talking on the phone. Not everyone is afraid of eating in public. Not everyone is afraid of attending parties. Not everyone is afraid of meeting new people. Not everyone is afraid of normal social interactions. Now everyone thinks I'm rude when I don't know how to socialize, it's one problem I've had trouble dealing with for years.

Dear Anonymous

I can say I feel you, because as a teen, and much younger, I didn't have much of a social life. No one knows why I didn't talk much, I just didn't. I had friends, just not like everyone else, who was friends with everyone, and liked by everyone. I was known, but for the fact I didn't talk, not because I was "cool". Looking back, not understanding why I kept so close and couldn't just open to anyone, to not talking to anyone and letting them bully me into believing I wasn't normal because I was so shy. Social anxiety, my mental health was out of control back then, but no one cared about your mental health then, some still don't, if so, no one would be bullied, or made to feel less than. That's why I learned it's important to take care of your mental health, and let the rest take care of itself. I took a step back and analyzed a lot of my life and the different stages I went through, and I realized I didn't miss out on the best school experience, I had that

experience. I had my few friends, the ones who were
real to me, at the point of my life I needed them. I
didn't need to be accepted by people who broke me
down to make themselves feel better, I might have
let them fool me into believing being a friend to
them might bring me out the shell I hided within,
but I'm blessed today, to know I didn't fall for
the insecure assholes who made me feel less of who I
was, completely losing myself because I thought I
needed to be better. I have always been humble. Your
mental health is important. And one thing to always
keep in mind when you look for someone to let in, if
they can't benefit to your being, they don't love
you the way you deserve to be loved, they're not
good for you, do what's good for you.

Anonymous 61

As a child, there was nothing I didn't have.
I used to have yearly trips with my parents to
exotic places. But I don't have a single picture of
me smiling. I never appreciated what I had. Maybe I
couldn't or maybe I didn't want to, maybe I wanted
something else. As a single child, I have dealt with
a lot of issues since my childhood, which I can
understand now, as a 21-year-old. I lived with my
parents in our hometown for years. My dad came home
from work on time almost every day. Just three of us
in the house and yet my dad was always watching tv,
mom in the kitchen, me doing anything but studying.
Even though I know some things about my mom and her
past. I wouldn't know anything about my dad if it
wasn't for the forms I had to fill sometimes. Not
even his full name. True story. My mom was like any

other mother obsessed with giving me food. But the thing with parents is that they try to impose their dreams and failures on their children. So unfortunately, she has trained me for dance, music and art. I appreciate that, now, but as a child, it was something I never wanted. I always wanted to spend time with my friends, but never got that. What I got was her taking her anger on me. Beating me black and blue. It was once each year, but the scars lasted long enough in my body and mind. I have tried talking about it with my grandmother or friends. All this made me want to run away and I already had estranged ties with my dad, which made me take college far away from home. I thought I was happy for three years, but all this trauma came hitting on me last year with severe depression. I didn't know who to blame. My mom brushes it off whenever I try to open. No other person will believe me if I said so and I am too afraid to go to a psychiatrist. Not because of medication, but because I wouldn't know what to do if it's true. I have tried so hard to keep everything pushed inside that I never thought I will have to face them one day. I thought I forgot all this. Today, all I think about is maybe if a younger me received a hug occasionally, some warmth, someone or anyone to talk with, a shoulder to cry on, I would have been a happier person. This is for the imaginary person whom I have already met or will meet someday:

> I hope that one day when we are together,
> There's no room to hide
> No time to play around
> No love that is unseen
> No voice that is unheard

And no space enough to feel distant
even a second.

Anonymous 62

I was 17 summer of senior year and trusted a
guy I never should' ve trusted. Known him since
middle school. He needed someone to talk to, me
being the person who likes to comfort people I
agreed to see him. I told my friend and she told me
to be careful, I didn' t understand why. I ignored
it, he started talking about how life has been for
him. He asked if I was a virgin. I replied with
"yes I want to wait until marriage" he said "I
can' t wait that long" in my head I was like, who
said I was gonna marry him, nothing else crossed my
mind. I trusted him. He knew I wanted to wait but he
didn' t care and that night he took that away from
me. A year ago, my neighbor, who I grew up with and
once trusted. He rang the doorbell and I told my
sister it was our neighbor, she told me to go open
the door for him, so I did. He walked into the house
without me letting him in and he asked if I was by
myself and I told him my sister was in her room. He
looked mad but I didn' t think anything of it. He
went to go sit on the couch and asked for a hug. I
knew this guy since we were little, so, I gave him a
hug. I pulled away and I asked if he wanted anything
to drink. He just looked at me and said "you' re
beautiful" I said thanks, he reached to lift my
shirt. That' s when I knew what was going on. I
pulled down my shirt and he said "come on, let me
see" my heart was racing. I ran to my sister' s
room and I told her he had to leave. I stayed in the

room shaking. I told my mom what happened, I cried to her. She still forgave him because "he wasn' t himself, he was on drugs" as if, that made it okay. It hurts. I spend nights crying trying to figure out why or who I did so wrong in life for this to happen to me. I get told to "move on it' s in the past" but it' s now become a part of me. It will always be with me till the day I die. I blame myself, because if I wasn' t nice and caring for others it could' ve been prevented. So now I struggle with anxiety, paranoia. It screwed me up. I just want to be the old me who was carefree and happy. But I don' t know how.

Dear Anonymous

The one thing you don' t do, is blame yourself for something like putting your trust into someone who you couldn' t trust. We have all put our all into someone, or more than deserved, just to get crushed and made out to the fool. Being open minded, full of love soul, sometimes you get lost within that love, and it makes it hard when the other doesn' t reciprocate that back, then when we get mistreated or disrespected, we blame ourselves, because we allowed it. One thing to always remember, your heart takes you through it, even the pain, your heart still makes it through. Don' t blame yourself because you loved too hard. Stop treating your heart badly because of the pain inflicted upon you, make that your reason to love harder.

Anonymous 63

I can't seem to move on from the man I love. He was my best friend. We laughed, we talked. He was the one person who was there for me through my anxiety, my family issues, everything. He kept leaving me. I would do everything and anything to have him stay he always left. He kept telling me we couldn't be together because of his family. Religion and family reasons, his parents would've never accepted me. There were times he'd come back and say, I want to love you, I want to feel love with you, then he left again. I kept thinking he would change. I can't get closure. I can't seem to get over him, after all that hurt. I can't get over him. I still think about him every day. I miss him all the time. I texted him and checked up on him, he said he was sorry for everything and he will never forgive himself and I told him, I forgive him, but I still love him more than I love myself. I can't get over him, and why I'll never understand why I couldn't be with the man I was in love with.

Dear Anonymous

The last line caught a piece of me, because I have too once never understood why I couldn't be loved the same way I expressed it, or why I was never good enough. I blamed myself because I misunderstood. I blamed myself because I loved them too blindly to see it was them. I once loved

someone, who never understood why I couldn' t be
with them, nor why they didn' t feel the connection
I felt. I was lost when it came to love, I ended up
disguising my love as lust, the need of wanting to
be loved, so, I fell in love with the idea. I
started to see the pattern I started with ones who
didn' t have much soul that matched with mine, maybe
just a good time, or lust I confused with love, and
ran with it and made it make sense, in my head.
That' s why I never thought I could blame them, when
I chose to let them keep repeating this pain. But I
couldn' t take the blame either, my heart is warm,
just because it' s been taken advantage of, doesn' t
mean I let it freeze. My love always remained the
same. My heart always ran deep. It wasn' t anything
about how I loved. One of the most difficult lessons
of love I learned, not everyone who speaks the words
of love don' t always feel it. Some are around to
love you, truly, then there' s some to teach you, so
one day you won' t choose the wrong one when it the
right time comes.

Anonymous 64

I feel like a dirty secret in plain sight.
I' ve been with my husband for 5 years, married for
2 come July. For years I' ve battled with my health,
had multiple surgeries on bowel disease and been to
hell and back. My husband always been my rock. 2016
we booked our wedding for 6 months' time then found
out I was pregnant. I walked down the aisle 5 months
pregnant and incredibly poorly. I was so poorly our
daughter had to come early via c section. I spent
every day with our newborn daughter thinking my
husband was working all the hours God sends to

support us. Wrong. When our daughter was 8 months old my world was destroyed. A strange woman messaging me to tell me she knew we were separated but he was suicidal, and could I help? What?! We'd never once separated and turns out he was depressed because he couldn't keep up with his web of lies. He'd been seeing a woman he was working with. He claimed we had separated, and he was living back at home with his mom. He told her he was going to push me under a bus and was only around for his daughter. Called her up to 10 times a day for 10 months and I didn't have a clue. When he was home from "work" he was the most loving husband in the world. All his lies began to be exposed. Our five-year relationship has been a sham. From day one he has been messaging 50+ women all with the same MO, he hates me and is not happy in our relationship. He tells them what a horrible person I am and says awful evil things duping them into believing he's so unhappy that it's ok for them to flirt and talk dirty to him. Turns out it's not them, it's me that's always been the dirty secret. He messaged filth to female members of my family, slept with a friend of ours, lied and cheated his way through life and I've been blissfully unaware. My trust in him has been my downfall because I've never once suspected, questioned or felt the need to check his phone. I thought everything was so perfect, we were the couple that everyone envied. We'd never once rowed, got married and had the most perfect baby girl. I feel like a fool. Yet stupidly I can't leave. I spend every single night torturing myself. Reading the screenshots of his cruel messages over and over. I don't know who this person next to me is. I've given him everything, a home, his daughter, I cook,

I clean, I even take care of his personal hygiene. I do everything, but still I wasn't good enough. He says I'm his world and his intention were never going to be to leave me, he just wanted attention. It's all on me, I'm not supposed to break down or think about everything he's been doing in the past because he's trying. I'm left having to deal with all this hurt anger and betrayal, but I'm supposed to make it work. I need someone to crack my chest open and take away my heart. Someone to take away this pain. I feel like I'm in a nightmare. My whole relationship has been a mirage. I feel trapped, but the only one trapping me is myself. I see the lies, I see the manipulation and how incredibly calculated he is, but I just can't let go.

Dear Anonymous

Wow girl, wow. I read that and my first thought was "she's strong". Strong because not everyone will sit around and get damaged after being confronted with what's next. My second thought was he has a serious commit problem, and I know you chose to blame yourself for this, when you stated you did "everything" to keep him, but he chose to search, and that's not your fault. It's not your fault some don't think what you give is enough, that there's something you lack, because if there wasn't, they wouldn't entertain elsewhere. The one thing that makes us lose ourselves is trying to understand why the other person chose the actions they did, and why they chose pain and not love they spoke of and faked, you'll always come up short. I don't have children, so my advice may not be

enough, but no child should have to see the pain in
the one who gave them life, kids are a reflection,
of every emotion you give off, it affects them too.
Everything you do around your child is a lesson, you
are their role model, the one person they trust
most, don't lose yourself in someone who could care
less if you fall. If they're not willing to pick
you back up after they let you go, that's a sign to
not look back. If they keep blaming you, for the
reason they chose to overlook you, that's a sign
right there to cut ties. No one who loves you will
ever make you wonder if they do. No one who loves
you will ever make you question your worth. Love
doesn't have attachments to pain, they don't come
hand in hand, but some may never bring you love,
some may only bring you pain. Please, don't label
that love. I once tried to understand why I wasn't
enough, without knowing I chose the wrong one. It
hurts because my heart was all in while there's was
occupied by someone who didn't do what I did,
that's when I understood it doesn't matter how
much you give, some will never feel it. To let go of
what passed and not open old wounds. We blame us so
we can still love them. Sometimes we even question
why we do, because all we receive is pain. All long
I was trying to prove my love I started to lose
touch on why I even did.

Anonymous 65

Three weeks ago, I broke up with my boyfriend
of four years and I felt relieved, relieved of the
heavy boulder I was carrying for the past couple
years. We started out okay, but as time passed, I
couldn't see the good in our relationship anymore.

He's a good guy, a funny and good boyfriend, but he's just not the one for me. I can't call him home, in his arms, in his eyes I can't see home. All I see is another guy who gives me so much stress. No comfort. So, after a year of trying to stretch our relationship, trying to give it all, trying to rip myself apart, trying to stay because you don't just leave a relationship when you're given hard times, I called it off. I ended it because I knew deep down it's just not going to work. He's not who I can see my future with. Whatever led me to the decision of ending my long-term decision is because of this one guy. This guy I also just met recently, this I guy that I know may not possibly treated me seriously, may have just been playing a "game" at that time I met him but at that very moment that I had that conversation in that room with him, that one night and day that I spent with him, something in me snapped awake. That night of talking about having sex, putting it off and talking about fears and dreams, he held me through my nightmares, stayed up with me, tried to understand me, hugged me while I fought my demons. It made me realize, things I was asking from my boyfriend wasn't hard to do, I was just simply asking the wrong person. This guy I just met made me feel like I was finally home. The way he held me in his arms, the way he looked at me it made me feel alive. I know I should be doing that for myself, and I am, but with him it was different. It took me sometime to accept my long-term boyfriend wasn't the one for me, to accept that I deserve better. That the number of years that you've been together counts but it's not the only thing to be considered. This one guy I just spent 2 days with compared to my 4 years made me whole. Made me find

myself, influenced me to burn brighter and brighter.
Right now, I find myself going back to that two days
than of my four years of memories for strength.
Currently I'm single and working on myself, loving
myself more, chasing my dreams and really making it
happen, doing things I want with friends and family.
Focusing on my career growth and just having fun. I
feel sad for my ex, especially when I remember that
he is a happy soul and I just did something to dim
the light in his eyes, I do hope someday we could be
friends, but never again will I bend and break, and
dim my light for someone else. As for the guy I met
I won't be seeing him for a while, I met him in a
different country and I won't go back to that
country anytime soon, so I wish him best and would
like to extend my love to him. Whether he knows it
or not he's given me something even I had a hard
time finding, myself.

Dear Anonymous

I found myself a lot in your story, it also
inspired me to write this piece. Your story isn't
asking for anything in return, as I see the beauty
in your story, and I admire it. I admire how brave
you were when it came to which direction to take,
and the road of you, you've chosen. I know you're
living a happier and less stress-free life, and I
pray you forever receive that energy, beautiful
soul. I found myself in this story, strongly. 2018
was the year my life changed in a different kind of
way. I was with someone for 4 years, I had the
comfort, I had the relationship, I had someone to
hold me at night, to make memories with. I had

someone to love me, like I always hoped. But after
almost 4 years I was faced with choosing us or
walking to find myself I lost when I chose to make
him love me. I should' ve known from the beginning
if you need to make someone understand how your love
is to be felt, it won' t be. I chased, I wanted to
be chosen. We lived a good life, in those years. But
like you said above, it came to its time. When that
day came, I would think of all the times I felt
empty, but never expressed it. I thought about all
the bullets I took when it came to us, giving up
myself to make us happy. I came to a decision there
was no real reason we parted ways, except it wasn' t
in the cards, any longer. I thought about holding on
and trying to find the void that was missing, but I
chose myself. Everything I chose after that decision
had the foundation it needed to be loved
unconditionally, because I had the power I did,
because I found the void, I was searching for in
myself. I' m in a happier place, I still hit a few
roadblocks but only to test my strength, to help my
growth. I was always someone who was terrified to
hurt another because of the pain I found myself in,
until it had to do with my happiness, and for the
expense of myself I would choose me all over again.

Anonymous 66

I became best friends with someone in college
through an ex-boyfriend of mine. I left the
boyfriend, changed schools, but kept him. We were
friends through it all: he lost his childhood best
friend in a motorcycle crash and I had a bad period
of depression that left me in a state where I was
ready to end it all. I talked him out of leaving

this world and being with his best friend and he
helped me see that life can be beautiful. We were
always there for each other, and he expressed his
feelings for me at one point. I couldn't even think
about feelings, this is my best friend, I can't like
him, I can't lose that friendship. For a very long
time, I pushed his feelings to the side, said I
couldn't see him that way. After having one of the
best, happiest, and most comfortable nights with
him, I started to catch feelings. I expressed this
to him, but I also expressed how I cannot lose him.
He was too much of an anchor for me, a rock of
stability in a world full of the unknown. I didn't
know what to do, on one hand this could be the
greatest love I could ever experience, on the other
hand if something goes wrong, I could lose him. We
talked and he had such comforting words, saying we
could try and see what happens and no matter what,
we would stay friends. He told me he can' t lose me
and doesn't want to. He would never want to risk
this friendship because of how grateful he is to
have me. If it does not go well, we go back to being
friends without any weirdness. I gave in, and taken
on romantic dinners for my favorite meal, watched
our two favorite hockey teams battle each other,
danced in Atlantic City. His family started to love
me even more. We spent New Year' s Day together,
introducing me to all his friends and getting drunk.
I was in a trance, there was so much love, so much
history, so many laughs, so much in common, so much
comfortability. He knew how to calm me down when I
get angry, he knew my favorite drink, my favorite
food, how to make me laugh, and he supported me no
matter what. Being with him was blissful, exciting,
and everything I dreamed of. I fell in love. The

only issue became the distance. We were two hours
away and lived different lifestyles. I was finishing
up my last year of college, stressing out over
school. He was working at a restaurant and enjoying
life whenever he could. We got into a fight over how
I ask him what he's doing too much, but that's
because I care about what goes on in his life and
how he's doing. He told me he doesn't like to go out
and text much because he feels rude to the ones
he's with, I would appreciate a text or call
letting me know that he'll be busy so I don't expect
to hear from him. He didn't understand. He thought I
was asking too much. I was his first real
relationship and he didn't know how to be a
boyfriend, so I was helping to show and teach him.
Suddenly, no answer. No response. I try again a day
later, no response. The fight wasn't that bad,
wasn't that big, wasn't something that even bothered
me much. I knew it had to be worked on, and I
assumed we would work through it. Two days later, I
send something else. No response. I am panicking, I
am scared, I am confused, I am unsure. I began to
worry and fear that either something happened to
him, or that this was it. I gave it a chance, and
something went wrong, and I lost him. The one stable
point in my life, ripped away. I don't know what I
did, I don't know what I said, I don't know how I
deserve what he did to me. I sent him a message in
the middle of a panic attack, he knows I have
anxiety and depression and I have a hard time
handling my attacks. Nothing. I reached out a week
later with a paragraph saying how I understand if he
got cold feet, how sometimes I can be a lot to
handle, but my door would always be open to him as a
friend. Nothing. Against my better judgement, I

reached out on all social media platforms thinking maybe something bad happened to him. I got blocked on every social media platform possible and got my phone number blocked. We never spoke again. To this day, I got no closure. I lost my best friend, and was left full of mistrust, confusion, and broken-hearted. They say it's better to have loved and lost than never to have loved at all, but here I am, still feeling the wrath of rejection and aftermath of heartbreak and wishing I never let it happen.

Dear Anonymous,

I've heard "I didn't get closure" many times, as well as I too, have said it, but look deeper, the closure is there. They left without no explanation, that's your closure. They chose to not speak a word on why, and that's what they'll have to live with, you shouldn't. They'll have to go on knowing they left you, and wonder what could have been. As you worry about what you did wrong, why you weren't good enough, they're thinking why they can't be, so they run. I've been victim, also played the role of the one who walked away without explanation, but my silence spoke everything for me. I thought about what it could do to them, but I remembered all the times they threw dirt on my name so carelessly, I didn't think my presence was wanted. I never reached out after I decided to leave behind the best friend, I loved for 7 years. I decided one day I wasn't going to text, I was tired of feeling less than I deserved. I was tired of being bullied by someone I loved deeply. I was tired of trying to make her love me the way I loved her, we were once best friends, but now we're strangers. It's been 2 years since I last spoke to her, not once has she reached out. I thought maybe she would reach out, after all the disagreements we had to me always recovering them when it wasn't always me, was draining. I was hurt she never chose to reach out, till this day I love her, praying she's doing well out in the world, sometimes I wonder if she thinks of me too, if she's praying for me too. I've come to a point of peace when I think of her, I'm not bitter anymore. I'm not angry. God has presented our friendship came to its end, and I had to make peace with it. I didn't get closure, because honestly, it never happens. No one "wins", one always loses. I don't believe in closure unless the closure is from within. It's your life, you make peace with the burdens you were dealt. To make sense of the reasoning others leave won't ever be fulfilled. Don't think because you chose to be more that's why your road came to an end, it's true, sometimes things aren't meant to be more than what they are, but sometimes, things happen in the exact way they're meant too, to show you why it wasn't meant to be.

Anonymous 67

I've been married for three years. I'm fiercely loyal, and we've been through a lot. Tons of distance, two deployments (he's military), and so much training I can't keep up with it. I married him when I was 19. We went to high school together we were friends and had dated once before. He's done so much for me, he's so supportive from a distance. But he does things that degrade me. My

ideas are always dismissed or degraded. Anything I
say must be corrected or rearranged by him. I've
gone to school, I've worked, I've taken care of
our house and animals all while he's gone. And
it's never good enough. He does nothing to help. He
pays his bills and that's it. I love him, and I'm
so worried about hurting him, but I'm finally
getting to the point where I am done. I feel
distant. I don't want to be with him anymore. And
we've talked about it. I've told him I can't do
this for the rest of my life. I can't. And he
started crying saying how he's not good enough for
me, and I ended up comforting him. Finding the
strength to leave him is hard, and he doesn't know
it, but I'm done letting him hurt me. I grew up in
a broken home. My parents have been divorced for 99%
of my life. My mom has gone through a lot of
"partners", and it's never been easy. She met my
stepdad when I was 10, and we moved in with him a
month after they met. They're still together, and
extremely abusive. In every way possible with each
other, and in most ways with us kids. I'm the
oldest, and I have three younger siblings on that
side. This past March, they were fighting so bad
that I thought I was going to have to drop out of
school, start working full time, and fight to get
custody of my siblings. My mom told me some nasty
things my stepdad said about me (even though I
haven't lived with them in 6 years) and it hurt.
But I was mostly mad because he said it in front of
my sisters. I told her I want nothing to do with him
anymore. But now they're getting along and acting
like nothing ever happened. My mom has been calling
me ungrateful, spoiled, and immature, because I
don't want anything to do with my stepdad. All I

wanted was an apology. I' m always there for her when they fight. And I get treated like trash when they start getting along. It hurts. It cuts deep.

Anonymous 68

I' ve been struggling a lot with grieving and death. I lost my dad not even 10 months ago and then my grandmother, I' m struggling tremendously. Some days are better than others, but I constantly feel anger and sadness, like I can' t seem to pick myself back up sometimes.

Dear Anonymous

I want to first say, the pain you feel won' t go away, but it will settle. Death is terrifying, it' s heartbreaking, and it leaves you with a hole inside your heart, that yearns for the love. We can' t always accept we can no longer see them, text them, call them, any of these we once took for granted, we now regret never doing it enough, may feel some guilt for not always being there, but always remember, this is life, you won' t always make someone happy, as they didn' t always bring you joy, but it was the balance that made it strong. We can' t guilt ourselves into believing we could' ve done more, when our loved ones know it wasn' t our decision. I' m a firm believer in fate, I believe everything happens for a reason, and not everything has a reason, but in the end it all ends in something to grow from. Death is hard to grasp when its someone we love, someone closest to us, someone who meant something deep. It doesn' t matter how, or

why, but trying to understand they're no longer
whole, is heartbreaking. I lost both my grandparents
and my cousin in the same year within three months
of each other, I was young, I fought the urge of
sadness even though I saw everyone around me broken.
I didn't face my emotions or find peace in their
separation from this world to the next, I hid the
pain. I lost a soulmate of mine two years ago, the
state of depression and stock I went in, was
something I couldn't explain other than the letters
I wrote her. I woke up every day going to work,
living my everyday life while masking the pain by
day only to be broken by night. I didn't think my
heart could hold all the pain I felt. I didn't
think my heart could handle what it was trying hard
to comprehend. I felt alone even when I had people
who loved me keeping me sane. I didn't think it was
fair her life was taken from her, that everyone who
loved her was now without her, and she didn't get
to stay longer. I was in shock. I cried an unbelieve
tears. I felt every emotion with every part of my
being, that's how I healed. She walked into my life
as the angel she was always meant to be, I loved her
so much, I know she knew. I found her soul
everywhere and that's what put my soul to rest. I
wasn't selfish any longer once she showed me the
way, when she taught me it's possible to keep
living, even after death, because we all go, some
before us which hurts, because we love hard and we
don't think it's possible to go on. Love and grow,
and let go, that's life.

Anonymous 69

A family that loves you, but so hard to deal with because of drugs and alcohol, I' ve raised my younger siblings. I' m 17 now, my mom' s in and out of jail currently there now, I' m trying to graduate but life throws all these things at me and makes it hard to focus on what I need done because I' m worried about other people, its caused problems in my relationship because I can' t focus or open up to him without wanting to cry he' s one of the only things that make me happy and I can' t even explain it to him.

Anonymous 70

I met my man online a year and 6 months ago, he's from Canada, I'm from South Africa. I fell in love with him before we met in person. I told him and showed him how much I love him, he booked a flight and traveled thousand miles to meet me, when we met in person, I felt complete till the day he went back to Canada. 2 months passed I applied for my visa to Canada it was denied. It's been 5 months now and I haven't seen him, we talk every day, but all I wanted and hoped for from him was to come and see me again since I have no access to his country but he can come to mine without a visa. I was broken and hopeless after the visa denial. I'm hopelessly in love with him, he loves me too. I just hope I won't get over him before he reads between the lines that I waited for him, if he doesn't come this month I'm letting go. I just need him next to me, a simple touch and a one more night would complete this void before I let go.

Anonymous 71

My ex caught feelings for another girl while we were dating and he left me for her, then came crawling back. While we were trying to work things out, he went and hooked up with another girl. I also just found out he's been sleeping with my best friend for about a year now. He doesn't understand why I can't forgive him, even if he builds my trust back. I felt worthless like I'm not good enough or never will be. I just can't trust him ever again. I have no confidence I feel like if he found someone better in the first place then he didn't really love me to begin with.

Dear Anonymous

Don't adjust your confidence because someone you loved chose to return that love in pain. If you gave what you had, without giving too much of yourself, it's not your fault. We can only do so much when it comes to loving someone and making them aware of the love you give. Your road with him ended the first time he left, letting him back in started the fire back up, and you burnt yourself. We've all loved someone and tried to make something right that wasn't meant to. We all loved someone and used that as an excuse to blame ourselves, as we forget we love ourselves too, and it's just as important. He's lost, he doesn't deserve you, and that's real to him, as he thinks if he keeps you hanging on one day, he may be right, but the constant pain repeated shows you why he's not. Don't let him define your worth, he's already proven his.

Write a letter to the you who wasn' t worthy,
tell us how you discovered your worth:

_____

_____

_____

_____

_____

_____

_____

_____

Insecurities are the scariest thing we hold
close to us, as we look at another soul and wish we
were like them, without even knowing their life. We
base off what we see on social media, and how they
project their lifestyle. insecurities come from a
dark place, a place where someone, once made you
feel like you weren't good enough. I once have felt
this, but there comes a time in your life where you
have to put things into perspective and see things
for what they are, and one thing for sure, you
can't want what someone has, or looks, because what
matters deeply is the soul that resides inside of
you: who you are is the most important lesson in
your journey and finding yourself is the hardest
part, because we base finding ourselves through so
many learning lessons in life, we want to be, and
want so many things that aren't meant to fit with
us because we want what makes others happy, or what
makes others want us, without realizing that's not
what makes us whole. if you're struggling to feel
good about yourself, I want you to look in the
mirror and say 1 thing you love about yourself and
do this every day. some may look in the mirror and

be unfamiliar with who they' re looking at, but some
may look and see themselves and realize they' re
chasing the wrong things, either or, everyone needs
to try this. I want to say, just because you' re not
skinny doesn' t mean you' re not beautiful and I' m
saying this because you don' t live to please
anyone, if you' re healthy, that' s all that
matters. if many are skinny and can' t gain weight,
some may want to be thicker, but at the end of the
day that you' re healthy is what' s most important.
Acne is one of my biggest flaws and I know how tough
it is to look at another with flawless skin and just
wish, but we were all made perfectly different, we
were all made to be what we are, don' t beat
yourself up because you don' t look like what
society tells you that you should. Don' t let
insecurities you create off being perfect drown you
into losing yourself. don' t let the insecurities
from anyone making you feel like you' re not good
enough stick around when you let that toxic person
go. You' re good enough. you' re beautiful.

I remember being lost without direction,
even my heart couldn't direct me to the destination
I was searching desperately for, because the
destination was out of reach and my heart couldn't
catch the grip, because my heart never knew the
difference between wrong and right, it loved whether
I was loved in return, or never done right. I held
connections close to my heart because it was rare
when I made any. I remember loving with all my
heart, but it longed for more, and the countless
times I overlooked that void because I thought they
made me whole. My heart couldn't direct me to the
destination I desired because I didn't know where I
am going. I remember loving, and being loved in
return, but not the way my soul felt whole. I loved
with my whole being no matter the situation I was
placed in, I gave all of me or none of me at all,
and some may see this as false, because in their
eyes, I walked away. In my eyes, I chose to step
away from their love, because their love wasn't
meant to hold my being at ease. I chose to walk away
because I knew we weren't meant to keep choosing
each other when we needed to choose to be a part. I
chose to separate the love from the toxic behavior
that kept repeating to open my eyes to the side

where I desired to be. I don' t regret loving anyone who held my heart in their hands and not in their heart, I will always hold those moments close to me because at one point they meant something more than this piece. I remember loving, and being loved in return, but I can' t remember loving myself enough. I can' t remember being strong to move closer to the destination my soul longed for, and after all these years, some may see it as time wasted, I see it as lessons learned. I see it as blessings that were missing. Looking back, I was afraid to find the destination because that meant change and there' s nothing, I feared more than change. Here I am, at that destination, and I couldn' t imagine fearing this feeling. I couldn' t imagine wanting to hide from this. Moral of the story, if you feel there' s more, don' t stay where you' re because you' re comfortable. Search for that special feeling, and don' t discredit how you get to the end, it' s the most important part of your story. You' ll get there, just once piece of advice, don' t regret. Don' t ever give up.

You were in love with illusion. An illusion
of someone you created off good characteristics and
some lust, as sometimes we confuse that with love,
because loving comes natural to us, and when we
love, we love hard. We convince our hearts that we
stick around after being blindly treated terribly,
and the misery that became our days, became our job
to fix—what we plant in our heads when it comes to
"being hard to love". No one is hard to love when
there isn' t anything hard about it, when you gave
all of you and never held back. The pain might sting
but when you truly step back and replay the
situation, you' ll see you' re not heart broken, and
you' re just hurt because what you thought was real,
wasn' t. And you' ll realize you' re loveable, and
to never let someone who doesn' t know their worth,
try and tell you yours. Don' t waste anymore lost
time being forgiving to them, forgive yourself for
dealing with their toxicity and love yourself enough
to not let them control you any longer.

To who loved someone but *never* felt **enough**:

People have a way of making you feel like you' re
not good enough, especially when it comes to being
loved. When someone doesn' t want you, the first
thing they latch to is "you' re not good enough"
or "you' re hard to love" which isn' t something
you should overindulge in, because the only bad in
the story, the only one who' s hard to love, is
them. You should never feel like who you are isn' t
someone to love, because when you gave your all and
opened your heart, even though they didn' t
reciprocate, that makes you strong. You aren' t weak
because you chose them before you, don' t make them
feel like what you gave wasn' t enough, you are only
capable of giving so much until you can' t anymore.

Note to self,

I won't let my self-doubts drown me; I won't let them define me of my purpose. I may not yet be where I'm destined, but I know this is only the beginning. I have many blessings that have already presented, and some, have yet to reach me, but I'm still praying. I won't give up, because this life I live is the only life I have, so I'll continue to pour into my cup, all in, and I'll forever be great. I'm speaking it into existence.

Dear Anonymous

I was someone who loved more, who always
wanted to show my heart. Not because I wanted to be
the one chosen, but because I was someone worth all
the love I gave. I never conditioned my love; I gave
but never pushed to receive. Instead, I conditioned
myself to believe if I showed my heart, and loved
wholeheartedly, the love will be reciprocated. But I
found myself in the circle of being the only one
loving. I searched. I chased. I tried to prove my
love to people who only wanted me to love them, but
never cared to express their feelings. Some want you
close so when they're ready to "settle down" you
might get chosen. My love wasn't a game, I wasn't
going to let someone who couldn't love me back,
play with my heart and try making me believe I
wasn't worth more. I realized I was important when
my heart was too big to love people who didn't care
to love me back. I went through a lot of
disappointments. I put myself in situations I
couldn't blame anyone else for the outcome. My
heart lived its own life, sometimes it was hard to
ignore the love that was beating. I loved people who

were wrong for me, and some who never loved me. I didn't wake up one day and "love myself" because to be honest, it's hard, to love yourself in a world filled with people trying to bring you down. The year of 2017 was a year that took a toll on my heart. I lost a close friend, it torn my heart apart. I learned how to cope with grief and moving on from someone I had no chose but to only love in spirit. 2017 was a year of learning how to love people from afar. I let go of a best friend I cherished for over many years. I became rocky with someone I was with for many years. I started letting go of people who didn't serve their purpose in my life any longer to become whole. I saw my worth after being blind for too long. I see why loving people who give me no purpose only made self-love further away. It took years of rockiness to let go of some people who were always on edge with my heart. It was hard because my heart loved so much, I didn't think it would be possible to look away from people I promised to love forever.

"It's okay, to outgrow the life
you thought you wanted"

I came across that quote today, and it
sparked something within me that I had to share. I
remember being happy within moments of my past with
people I thought I'd love forever. If you were to
ask me a year ago, I'd probably tell you I was
going to love the same souls until forever, or that
my soul finished searching. But a year later, I have
a completely different life, and a completely
different future planned, so I couldn't. That's
the importance of living in the moment, you don't
think whether you're going to want more, or outgrow
the life you had, or the love you thought would
never die, but that's where we go wrong. I was
happy in the moment. I loved in the moment. I gave
my all in the moment. I was honest, real, and raw to
nothing less than the heart I have, and the love I
always gave was unconditional because the
relationship I always promised was never dishonest.
I might have said things, done things, but mistakes
helped me understand the importance of love. I never

hurt anyone the way they hurt me, until they decided to show I was worthless. I never chose to walk away until they showed me which direction to take, I didn' t even see the door until they pushed me towards it. The thing about me, is when I open myself to someone, I give everything without holding back, because how do you love only in half? I couldn' t. I let people choose whether they could break me, I made it possible. I don' t regret the love I gave, or received, because I know I only did right by everyone I let love me. I' m sorry, if you' re hurt now that I chose to walk away, and chose to love me instead, or if the pain of me no longer loving you as I promised, forever. I would just like to say, I' m not sorry, I gave you everything I had in the moment we had, but what I gave wasn' t supposed to stay if I promised. We grow, and that' s important to remember because not everyone will be someone in your life forever, and you will outgrow what you loved, or once wanted, but that doesn' t make you a burden.

A lot of us weren' t taught self-love, we were taught to love another unconditionally, or that someone else is more important, which isn' t true. The only way to give your all to someone else is to love yourself and set the foundation. There' s no map of self-love, it' s just no longer putting up with the same pain, and walking away from people you once loved. It' s a lot of love lost, but you gain understanding and love within yourself no matter the time.

I believe we have many soulmates throughout our lives, in all forms; friends, lovers, family, and some who are stopping by. You create beautiful connections with beautiful souls throughout your life and won't realize it completely until you remember the memories, as you replay them to remember the good, they brought to you. Soulmates will never be forgotten; their vibe was a vibe you never felt until they helped you feel. Soulmates bring a piece of us without realizing, some are just around to teach us many months or years of joy, to resulting into pain or confusion, some were only around to teach you a lesson. Soulmates are around to keep us believing in love, friendship, or a good person. Not everyone you come across is a soulmate, don't try making everyone a soul-mate connection. When you feel it, you can't deny it, even if it ended, the way they made you feel, and the connection never left. Not everyone is meant to be around for as long as you planned, some are our control, as some aren't, but both have reasons and sometimes those reasons aren't clear to us. We need to trust, pray, and love. Let people love you. Let yourself love. Don't be afraid to open your heart to people because they can end up a moment, that one moment could be the rest of your life.

We all make it through. I myself thought I
was broken, then I wrote this whole book to tell my
story how everyone else around me made me feel like
I was, but in fact I never was. Damaged, lost, not
whole, but never broken. Every day is another day to
keep going, the hurt you feel may last for a while,
but the longer you dwell in the pain and the loss,
the longer it will hurt. Everyone experiences pain
in different ways because we all feel differently,
but one thing for sure, we all heal, but it' s up to
you to let yourself.

Sometimes you need to be selfish, especially when people don' t bring you anything, but instead hold you back. You meet some selfish people, who don' t want you to grow, and will pray on your downfall. These people are always people you love and sadly, we outgrow people we once loved. Not promoting abandonment. I never once said I didn' t love them, but there comes a time where love isn' t enough. If someone makes me choose between my dreams, desires, and them, I' m sorry but I' m always choosing me. If they loved me, they wouldn' t make me choose.

Anonymous 72

Just a couple months ago I went through a rough breakup. He didn't feel things anymore, but I still felt everything. I loved him with my whole heart. A couple months after we broke up, we didn't talk but I still wanted him back so badly and I missed him dearly. I vented to a lot of people including my closest family member. My 14-year old cousin. She was like my little sister and I could tell her everything we spent so much time together. I eventually found out that my cousin and my ex had sex. The day I found out I had the worst panic attack of my life. I never felt more betrayed. She admitted to it and my whole family found out. As for him he tried denying it still. Eventually he admitted it when he found out I had proof. To this day I never got an apology. I never felt so betrayed and it's hard for me to move on. It's now been 9 months and I'm not sure how to move on, or to let go. I reached out to my cousin and I could tell her apology was not sincere. It's like she was forced to say sorry. How do you move on from betrayal? How do I move on from thinking I did something wrong for them to do this?

Dear Anonymous

First, ask yourself one question, do you really believe it's something you did? Why would you be to blame? We often blame ourselves when someone sends heartbreak our way, because we feel we could've done more, or could have changed the way they felt, but in all honesty, you can't change what someone decides to do. Long as you were loyal, played your part in the relationship, and like you said, loved wholeheartedly, you can't put the blame on you. We need to start taking better care of ourselves when it comes to getting our worlds torn apart. We need to start looking at the bigger picture. It's not always about what you did that made them betray you, but more so, there may not be a reason, just their own selfish ways. The universe looks out for you in situations like these, it takes what's bad for you, right out of the story. Sometimes it's as simple as that, what's not meant for you will be separated from you, it's just up to you to handle the situation at best, and not let it destroy you.

Anonymous 73

Along the lines of feeling like an oddball, and inferior to others, I've made it my mission to make sure anyone I love is protected. Maybe the love is too much, or maybe I don't know how to manage and balance the time I give others and myself. I fear losing the ones I love the most to it. Sometimes I spiral out carelessly and people get tired of me being a mess, they leave without notice. In my life from bullying to failed relationships, I just wonder why? Why did this start? Why does it happen? What do I do to fail? Maybe there is no real answer or good one, so now I strive to continue to stay true to loving others and trying the best to love myself.

Dear Anonymous

One thing I learned in my 20's, it doesn't matter how much you love them, if you don't love yourself more, you will always lose that love. You may protect the love with every part of your being, but it will always be lost. Firstly, you need to condition the love you have for others, by loving yourself first. You can't give someone everything they need if you can't give yourself what you need. I also, was bullied growing up, because I didn't talk, and everyone used that as an advantage to use against me. I learned one thing about every bully, they don't love themselves, the most insecure. Back then, I let them get to me, I let them win, I lost my voice within. But now, I know how weak they were, and now I'm praying they have found that love they desperately needed, the love they torn me down to receive. Bully's don't define us, instead, they make the road to self-love more difficult, because we lose all hope in ourselves by their comments. I remember caring what everyone thought of me. I remember wanting to be understood, until I realized there's no making them understand. Self-love is the hardest chapter in your life to uncover, it's hard trying to love yourself in a world full of roadblocks, dead-ends, and constant reminders how you can fail at any time. One thing to always remember, no one is you, and no matter how hard the journey to loving yourself is, you'll always make it.

Anonymous 74

When I was six, I was molested for the first time. My aunt is an addict and left me outside a bar. I was so young I had no idea what happened to me, not until it happened again at 7 when my aunt sold me for a bag of cocaine. Again at 9 and 12 I was raped by my aunt's "friends" for years it haunted me and instead of handling it. I began an eating disorder, depression, and anxiety. It wasn't until I was 20, I began to figure out everything that happened to me. I was rapped for the very last time. He was a stranger, who came into my apartment and took advantage of me. Using hate and anger as a tool to tear me apart. It was violent and something out of a nightmare. I spent two weeks in the hospital, four days in the ICU and after that months upon months in court where I was asked "what did I do to provoke him" and "if I could have done anything differently" as if I asked for it all! He got 65 years and I finally got peace. In that time, of me going to court, I met a wonderful man. At first, I was terrified, not knowing how to trust him or what he would think of me and my past. All I've known of men is hate and being used. Besides my father, every man has abused me. When I met my now boyfriend, I was terrified. I told him everything, realizing he deserved to know why I have nightmares and why when he touched me, I shuttered. He cried, and instead of asking why or anything else, he pulled me onto his lap and allowed me to cry. He cried along with me as I released every bit of anger and doubt. From then on, he asked before touching me, he holds me at night when memories comes along, and he makes sure I know I am loved. I never knew what love was until my man came along. He has shown me what love is, and has shown me how beautiful I am. Because of him I see how amazing I am, how smart, beautiful, strong, silly, everything I never saw before. Because of him I long for kisses, I want to be touched, I know what making love is like and what sex was intended for. Two people expressing the ultimate form of love. Because of that man and everything I have been through. I am the woman I am today. And I couldn't be happier, and proud, to be in love with a real man.

Dear Anonymous

I can't lie and say I feel your pain, because I'm trying to imagine but instead, my heart breaks a little more as I kept reading. I know my heart can't say sorry enough, even though you may hear those words a lot. I'm sorry you were brought through life having the wrong idea on what it's supposed to be like. I'm sorry you never felt any love you deserved, instead, the word love became lost and the word peace made more sense, as you chased for peace, I'm proud of the strength you have. Someone who has been through what you have, and to make it through, to be able to love someone, while fighting those demons. I believe it's not easy, I believe it still hurts. Sometimes I wonder why life takes us through the worst possible situations, to just test our strength, it never makes any sense. But after all the abuse, and all the pain, you found your way out, you found your peace. You were set free from the situation, but those memories will forever haunt you. My heart is happy you were able to move forward and find a man who could show you the ways of love, and the importance of love. I pray you can one day detach from everything that you thought defined you and create your real purpose. I pray you always feel what real love is, you deserve every ounce of it.

Anonymous 75

At the age of 1, my family is my world.
The age of 3 I was diagnosed with autism.
The age of 5 I started coloring with my imagination.
The age of 6 kids in school started teasing me.
The age of 7 I had problem studying and paying attention in school.
The age of 8 art and tennis became my passion.
The age of 9 my parents transferred me to a new school, no one wanted to be my friend.
The age of 11 I had a crush.
The age of 13 kids bullied me.
The age of 14 I started high school and became the outcast.
The age of 15 I fell in love with the only boy who genuinely liked me in school.
The age of 16 I was heartbroken.
The age 17 I experience depression, graduated high school, and began college.
The age of 19 I found my true friends, also had my family.
The age of 20 I became an animator, coach, student educator, model, family woman, socially open, capable, confident, and a self-loving person.

"No matter how much I struggle or grow in life, I am still learning how to beautiful I am, inside and out"

(Fill the years that lead to your growth)

The age of 1: _____

_____

The age of 2: _____

_____

The age of 3: _____

_____

The age of 4: _____

_____

The age of 5: _____

_____

The age of 6: _____

_____

The age of 7: _____

_____

The age of 8: _____

_____

The age of 9: _____

_____

The age of 10: _____

_____

The age of 11: _____

_____

The age of 12: _____

_____

The age of 13: _____

_____

The age of 14: _____

_____

The age of 15: _____

_____

The age of 16: _____

_____

The age of 17: _____

_____

The age of 18: _____

_____

The age of 19: _____

_____

The age of 20: _____

_____

I am _____.

I love _____ about me.

I need to _____.

I' m still _____.

Anonymous 76

I was in a relationship with a narcissist. I left him in January after three years. Throughout the time period he would invalidate me, always look at me with no expression when I would cry, and yell at me when I was upset about something he did. He would tell me that it would take a long time for him to find me amazing, hide that he was talking to other girls, and get so angry and call me crazy if I found out. The minute we break up, he writes to some random girl saying that I'm psycho and I'm a horrible person. He convinced her he's hurt and broken because I'm so evil, and of course she believes him. He continues to talk about me to everyone. However, through the last three months of our relationship, I was preparing to leave. I read books on narcissism and everything just started to make sense. When I finally left it was amazing. I feel so happy. I used to cry every single day because he made me feel worthless and said no one else would love me like he did. Which was all lies because I could find someone that respects me and cares about my feelings more than he ever could pretend to. I spent three years with his stupid ass and now I'm finally free. I wish people knew what he was. He puts on a show and makes everyone think I'm the horrible person. It has made me stronger, helped me know my worth and respect myself, as well as not

caring about what people think of me. If they judge
me without knowing me or the situation, that's up to
them. I'm so frustrated with myself I let myself be
treated badly for 3 years, even though I knew things
would never change. Promised he would change, and I
was the love of his life, then continued to make the
same mistakes and get mad at me. Towards the end he
became so evil and cold and would not let me feel
bad ever. If I did, he would call me names and the
fact that I wasn't okay with him sleeping over with
girls was why he thought I was controlling and
ruining his life. I'm just so happy he is gone out
of my life. I feel so stupid. I know I've learned so
much, but I wasted three years. I could've learned
all this within a year, but I always made excuses
for him because I thought I loved him. Turns out I
didn't, only the fake version of him I created in my
head from all the sweet talk. It's so frustrating, I
just wish everyone knew what he was like

Dear Anonymous

You put your all into someone you loved, and
you were clueless on why you even did, when you
think of it now, right? Because I feel that. See the
thing about love, is when we love intensely, but
sometimes loving intensely can get the best of us,
not only in a good way. We let love become a weapon
to us, we become blind by who we fall in love with
because we attach why we want to love to anyone, and
say we love them. You'll see the difference in the
two kinds of love when you realize you're loving
them and not trying your hardest to prove that love,
when it's real love, they'll feel it as much as
you. There's ups and downs, but no one who truly

loves you will ever hurt you and make you believe
you' re someone who' s hard to love. People like us,
with good hearts, we let love not only a good drug
to us, we also let it kill us. You' ll learn if you
didn' t know what love isn' t, you' ll never
appreciate what love truly is. You' ll never
understand the real if you couldn' t compare the
fake. Everything you go through in life is a lesson
we all need to find the parts of us that are still
hidden. We learn new things about others every day,
just like we do about ourselves. You need to accept
not everyone' s meant for you, they' ll be ones who
will only be out to hurt you, that' s the role they
play in your life, don' t change that. Don' t keep
loving people who don' t deserve to. Don' t surround
yourself with needy people who only drown you into
darkness.

Anonymous 77

I was in a relationship for 1 year and 5
months, it consisted of laughs, and arguments
majority on my part because my communication was not
great, but I learned to be better at it. He broke up
with me once because of a mistake I did, then we got
back together. He broke up with me again, and we
both were at fault. He loves me but doesn' t want a
relationship. I told him to consider it or a least
think about it. I reached out but he doesn' t
answer, I decided to stop reaching out I' m just
afraid I guess.

Dear Anonymous,

You can't force to love someone you weren't meant to love, or the other way around. It's easy to attach loving someone and reasons why you shouldn't let go—but know you're attaching yourself to the right kind of love, and not trying to make someone love you. Weigh out the good and the bad, ask yourself if you believe this is something you want forever, because if it's not, you shouldn't keep indulging in it.

Anonymous 78

I'm trying to get over a mentor, who used to be my manager and now is a dear friend, super important to me. We have been intimate, but we haven't made it a thing because he has a girlfriend, an open relationship and I want more. It's very hard to hang out without starting something and I've tried to control myself but the connection I feel we have is real. As I type this, I feel silly about it, describing it like this, but the reason any of this happened is because I really feel like we are meant to be together, but the timing is off. I just got a new job and I'm upset thinking about not having that connection with him anymore. I'm also excited because maybe this is what I need to give me some space and distance from him. I know we will be together. But later in life.

How can someone move on feeling this way and still attract the "right kind of love" and relationship we deserve? He's an amazing person, but we are at totally different stages in our lives. He's lived a life already and I'm still in my "prime" years, so he can't give me what I want now and we both know it. Letting go and knowing I will fall in love, a different love, it's so scary and I almost want to say heartbreaking, how does this exist?

Dear Anonymous

When I first fell in love, or the love I thought I fell into, I believed in right person wrong timing, but now, I believe there's no such thing. Right away, the connection will tell you how the rest will go, and sometimes things change terribly, that's just your road coming to an end. Forcing a connection that ran it, course will only hurt you, it will never make you feel like you need it. If that person was meant for you, the time would be that time, it's only when you choose to overlook the signs of them not being the one, which will drive you to believe they will always be right for you, and find every excuse to believe it's true. Most of the time we meet people and make connections that are unforgettable, but some were only meant to be a quick lesson. That's why it's important to not attach love to every connection, or a mess will be made everytime. Learn the difference between love, and lessons, love that's forever won't make you think twice. Love that's for the moment will always give you energy that doesn't match up, and if you confuse the two that's when heartbreak comes to play you as the fool.

Anonymous 79

I met this kid when I was 15, he was 17. We were in high school and we were together for two years. Over the first six months things were going perfect, you know we were obsessed with each other, then he had to move back to Texas, and I wanted to end the relationship, but he cried, to me that he wanted it to work. The day he left he gave me "rules" that included cutting off all my male friends and not talking to guys unless I absolutely had too. When he was a way in Texas he had a whole new girlfriend, I didn't find out about until a year later but he would tell her I was crazy and hacked his Instagram, and blocked her when really he did it so she couldn't see pictures of me and him. He came back in October, that's when we made our first year together and the first thing he said to me when we saw each other was that I was a lying dirty hoe, and he needs to see my phone and make sure I wasn't talking to other guys. He wouldn't let me touch his phone at all, he stayed til February and lived with me and my mom, then went back to Texas. I was desperate to keep what we had going because I cared so much for him, he would control me 100% he had all my social media passwords but would log me out of his all the time by "accident" and he told me, if I didn't send him nudes he would need to find other girls to satisfy his needs he put us on breaks constantly but when I would try to move on he'd call me at 3am crying about how bad his life is (he was a drop out with no goals) and I felt bad, and would come crawling back to him. In April, I paid for him to come back to see me for my 17th birthday, since I had practically no friends because he made me drop so many people, he didn' t trust I wanted to have him around. He would use coming to see me as a threat whenever he thought I was doing something sneaky. When he came back; he was different, more aggressive, would push me around. I found out all the girls he cheated on me with, at this point I felt so low about myself because they' re all so beautiful and I didn' t think I was because he' d tell me I wasn' t good enough to please him. I stayed with him because I was scared to be alone, I had no friends, he was the only person I had around, besides my mom and brother. I was depressed, I had to go to the hospital due to not eating or sleeping, I went from 110 pounds to 84 pounds in two months. My senior year of high school I started sneaking around his back and talking to my old guy friends, but he found out and that' s when he punched me in the face, thrown me to the ground and kicked me around. He' d force me to have sex with him, then not speak to me for weeks. Everything was on his terms and I was just there for him when he was bored. I tried leaving once and that' s when he got the worst and started strangling me and beating on me saying if I loved him, I' d know he' s hurting me out of love. Basically, he cheated on me the last time and I left him. I got a restraining order put on him, he still reaches out to me asking for forgiveness to this day the whole thing made me feel so worthless and scared to be with anyone. I always felt like I wasn' t good enough for someone to care for.

Anonymous 80

There is this guy I love very much, but he's
not meeting me halfway. The last time I complained
about him being distant he told me he's busy at a
cousin's wedding and I should give him time. We work
together. Do you think this guy still loves me? He
was gone for 2 weeks. In that time, he only talked
to me once, he came back yesterday. I don't know
how I feel about him now. I wasn't that excited
about seeing him yesterday. I was okay. I think
I've accepted he's not that into me. What's left
is for me to let go.

Dear Anonymous,

The heart will always know what it knows and
feel what it feels. Your love will always remain,
but you'll accept and realize what really is, and
what's not and put into play what need to happen,
letting go is what's best. Don't let old flames
linger around you with vibes you wouldn't give to
another.

Anonymous 81

I've been in relationships that doesn't
always go the way I want it to go, I'm a really
private person and tend to separate myself whenever
I feel ignored or unwanted, or when it comes to my
emotional problems and past so last year I meet some
"great friends" and started hanging out with them
this year and opened up to them and they were like

"we'll always be by your side". I have a tendency of whenever I feel depressed, I post a sad quote or and they never respond, or they never ask me what's wrong or how I'm doing. I also feel ignored most of the time so I got tired of them never caring and they always came to me for advice so I posted that I'm tired of ppl never caring about me so I'll never listen to their problems again, that's when they decided to ask me what was going on, I got mad and left them on read. I just ignored and they kept texting me asking me what was "wrong". It's been less than 2 weeks I've been focusing more on myself and letting go of negative people, but I feel guilty I left without a trace is it, should feel guilty or should I go back to them?

Dear Anonymous,

You aren't wrong to ghost people, especially if you've explained yourself time and time again. Regardless if it was about them or someone from your past, we all have a story about how someone hurt us, we reflect that onto everyone else and expect them to understand to not hurt us. Regardless what you tell someone, we're all human. No one will always do you right, and sadly, you need to let those people go. The more you chase someone who doesn't want to be chased, you'll find yourself in the same situation. So, you're not wrong, you're not wrong to just let go of things or people if you honestly believe there isn't anything more. If you feel the need to explain yourself and why you let them go, you may do that also, just be prepared you might never get the answer you want, the apology, or forgiveness. Approach this with an open mind, not a heavy heart, you' re just looking to hurt yourself.

Anonymous 82

I' ve recently been going through a long-distance relationship and things have been kinda hectic for me. I feel like I' m starting to get over it, but some nights I feel like I' m back to where I started. I just need some words of wisdom and motivation for moving on.

Dear Anonymous,

Long distance relationships aren' t easy, I use to love them when I was younger until I realized it gave them a reason to have a whole another life without me. When love is involved, it takes a while to come to a point of no return. But when you find peace in leaving and you feel there' s nothing left to give, you' ll feel it. It takes time to heal wounds that are so deep. Just remind yourself there is no good in something that makes you feel otherwise.

Anonymous 83

My "best friend" slept with the guy that dumped me, the night after. I felt like I wasn' t good enough because I' m not a size 2 or perfect.

Dear Anonymous,

The thing is, sometimes we get caught up in how we feel and forget theirs, and what they want. We create an illusion on what we want and not even think twice. Then sometimes, others have a way of making you love them and leaving like you were nothing and lead you to somewhere you can't explain the feeling, but you'll feel it. We sometimes want the things that don't want us most of the time and it doesn't make sense. You can't make someone like you whether it's your physical beauty or your inner beauty, neither change when it comes to them, how they see you, how they feel about you is their view. You will always be beautiful, your heart will always be pure, that's beauty. Don't let dark times change the light on your beauty.

Anonymous 84

Recently just got out of a toxic relationship and have finally had the realization I should cut ties, that he's no longer good for me, but I'm unsure how to take the step from wanting to let go, to actual letting go.

Dear Anonymous,

Toxic people are called toxic mainly because they're so good at faking, and making you love them through their two faces. It's hard to let go of

people who you've grown so close to, let your heart
open love to. The hardest part is letting go,
especially when you want to desperately hold on, but
you know you'll break, don't think twice, just go.

Anonymous 85

To appreciate goodbyes, and to acknowledge
that when you love and invest in someone your
proving to yourself how much you're capable for
someone and that identifies you they someone else.

Dear Anonymous,

When you love someone, you love them, like
your whole heart loves them without thinking twice.
It doesn't matter the relationship or friendship
love is love and the people you love will be
important in your life. Just like you were meant to
meet people, you were meant to tell some goodbye, it
might sound difficult to say goodbye to someone you
thought you'd never have to let go of, but
honestly, there are so many roads out there, some
people can't decide which road to take, and when
they do, you might not take the same one and don't
ever let anyone make you feel the way you choose to
grow is wrong, that who you are is someone
unfamiliar. No one can identify you as someone
you're not, who you are will always be real when
you give your heart, especially to people who only
give you their time. Appreciate the good in
goodbyes, like you appreciate the first glance, both
will tie into how you find yourself.

Anonymous 86

I had been dating this girl for almost 6 years, on and off always taking her back knowing there was not going be no difference but hoping there would be. She was never faithful, always lying and proving me right Last couple of months of being together I felt disgusted, hatred, and sadness being with her, but I kept her around. She was manipulative, really had a hold on me. I didn' t know how to let go, I also loved her. She let me go. She cheated on me again and left me for that girl. I' m just all mixed emotions but a big huge weight has been lifted off my shoulders.

Dear Anonymous,

From my view, you have no choice but to let go, not saying it will be easy, but you said everything you needed to hear. She played games with your heart and you kept going back, which isn' t wrong because good hearts don' t walk away when times get rough, they stick around and get hurt over and over but remain whole. You can' t stay forever, especially when you' re being treated less than you deserve, but won' t know what your worth if you drown in the sorrow of losing someone who didn' t want to keep you. She didn' t choose you, this will all be a blessing once you see it. It may take a while for you to understand, but everything happens for a reason, she showed you what love wasn' t, your soulmate is still out there.

Anonymous 87

How do we move on from someone who we really love? He always makes me happy, but when he's no longer around everything I'm a mess. I just don't know where to start.

Dear Anonymous,

The first step is finding the comfort in yourself, being able to be alone. You need to find comfort in not needing someone else, not needing someone to make you happy. Happiness from everyone else will only be temporary if you can't be happy with yourself. Moving on from someone you love deeply is hard, it could take some time, but if you follow the signs, if you open your eyes and see the message in front of you, you'll be able to go on. Your heart isn't broken, it might seem hard to breathe but sometimes our hearts are prepping for heart break, but heart break is so much worse. Thinking about letting go can break your own heart. Don't over think, only make decisions on what's real and what's right there. Focus on you and realize your worth before you love someone else, or nothing will make sense.

Anonymous 88

What do you think or feel, when someone tells you love is blind?

Dear Anonymous,

Love isn' t blind, at least to me it' s not.
I can truly tell you when I' ve felt love, real
love, there was nothing blind about it, I felt it
immediately after facing it. I do agree that people
can let love blind them, using love as an excuse to
let no good people keep destroying them.

Anonymous 89

I' ve been with this guy on and off for three
years and we talked about living together, he' s
deployed right now so I was going to wait for him.
Today he called me and asked me "do you see us
together in 5 years" I said "yes" he said, "to
be honest I really don' t and I think we should
break things off" now I feel empty, 3 years of my
life was for him. He' s really gone. If we do get
back together it won' t feel the same because of the
pain I felt when he told me he doesn' t see us
together in 5 years, so what' s the point? I put up
with a lot because I want him to be my person, I
want him in my life. The heart wants what it wants,
and I want him, but if it' s not for me, then it' s
not for me.

Dear Anonymous,

I don' t believe in on and off, nothing in
the end, ends up as happily ever after, honestly.
You can' t force love in places it will never be no
matter how much you love someone. Sometimes people
go different roads and expect you to always love

them, and if he wants you to wait for him that's not fair to you. You don't know what he's doing there and it's going to cause more upsetting nights than you're living now. Someone who can tell you straight up they don't want to be with you is a sign right there. You need to find a way to cope with how you feel and move on. Focus on yourself and loving every part of you, you'll be able to love someone else with the same love you give yourself.

Anonymous 90

The impact a toxic relationship has on you after you get out of it. I am currently in the best relationship I've ever had. But before that I dated guys who abused me mentally and physically. Which led to PTSD and made my depression worst. Made me value my worth. And how important it is to educate yourself and be willing to grow and better yourself after no matter how hard it gets.

Dear Anonymous,

It's important to relive every situation you've ever went through, through memories of course. It's important to take the good and realize how it's helped you grow, and to also take the bad, and realize how it made you into who you are without them. The first step to letting go of toxicity is to understand what about someone makes them toxic. You need to fully accept you can't change or make someone ever love you, who wasn't meant to feel that intimately with you. Some people weren't meant to love you, they were meant to stop by and teach you the someone you don't need anyone, they teach you how important being comfortable in your own solitude is, yet getting you ready to love the person you were meant to give your all too. It comes down to you, toxic people can only keep intoxicating you if you let them—show them you've always been better without them, while loving yourself beautifully.

Anonymous 91

Seeing my sister constantly go back to the guy that was inconsistent and selfish. He always tried to sabotage her by texting her after ignoring her for weeks saying he was depressed. She would get up without hesitation knowing she had to be up for school at 7 a.m. to go be there for him and come home at 2-3 a.m. All he ever wanted was her body. It hurt so much seeing how blind the love she had for him had her doing things out of the ordinary when he wouldn't even break a sweat for her. But thank god she doesn't deal with that anymore. It makes me happy and I'm not hurting no more seeing her in that situation. All good energy.

Dear Anonymous

You can't make someone see the pain they love, it will take a lot of time, but it will all come to light. We all need to learn, some of us just get burned too many times before we learn.

Anonymous 92

My ex-boyfriend was toxic. Or maybe we were. We never met eye to eye on anything. We dated for a year. Everything was great at the beginning. Then he stopped doing everything he did at the beginning of the relationship. Whenever I would bring up something that bothered me, he'd call me "crazy". Sometimes if our arguments were bad, I'd get called a bad name. Or he'd tell me that I'm "stupid or dumb, little to no brain". Other times, he'd yell at me and he would say he never loved or cared about me, then 10 minutes later he would tell me he only said that to get to my head and that he didn't mean it. Last August, he was going through family issues and he stopped talking to me for 2 weeks, no explanation or anything. I called him once, he yelled at me, calling me "needy" and told me to fuck off. I also sprained my ankle during those two weeks, and he knew but didn't bother to ask if I was okay. Towards the end of our relationship I told him I felt alone, like I wasn't dating anyone. He said that he isn't the "loving" type and that there's no need for me to need constant reassurance. I guess a small part of me hopes he comes back, but I know he won't.

Anonymous 93

Long four years of disloyalty and fighting to feel like number one in his life. He moved out two weeks ago and hasn' t been the same with me. He does work OT but I feel like there' s a disconnection I addressed it and we fought, then ended up at the same club and his baby mother did as well And she tells me that' s why I was having sex with him 2 days ago.

Dear Anonymous

You shouldn' t have to fight to be anyone' s number 1, you either are already or never will be unfortunately, and I know when someone has kids it' s different, but in that case you do as well, so you know your kids come first. But as a lover, friend, and everything more, you should always come first, you shouldn' t have to feel like you' re fighting for a spot you should already occupy. I' ve never been in a relationship with someone who has a child, so I can' t speak for the baby mother, but I' ve heard sometimes there' s connections that are left unfinished, which makes it easier to go back because toxic behavior loves its company and that' s all that is, there' s no love found, just easy to go back. You' re searching for more and wanting more, after those long years you deserve more honestly, don' t settle just because you have history, that' s the worst possible thing to do. If you' re not being treated like you deserve, and nothing is being reciprocated, don' t stick around.

Anonymous 94

It seems that I'm loving toxic people all the time because I was ignoring the toxicity in myself. This person was toxic because they were always depressed, using my love for him as a tie to keep the cycle of "I wish I was better for you" going. I'm releasing him now because I can no longer take that with me.

_____

_____

_____

_____

_____

_____

Anonymous 95

Why is it so easy to fall for the ones who treat us badly while we find the ones who are full of love, annoying?

_____

_____

_____

_____

Why are we so easy to go back to the people who hurt us but get mad at the ones who don' t?

_____

_____

_____

_____

Why are we so quick to hate on ourselves but love someone else? Why can' t we accept our own flaws, but we can accept others? Why can' t we learn to love ourselves the way we wish others would?

_____

_____

_____

_____

_____

Anonymous 96

My boyfriend had this female friend that he used to "mess around" with before me. He doesn' t speak with her or anything, but recently, he posted on snapchat a video of his brother' s dog and she commented on them. I feel a bit insecure about her randomly commenting, and it just makes me feel some type of way. I did bring it to his attention, but he just assures me that there' s nothing there. For the past 2 days I' ve been having reoccurring nightmares with her in them, and I don' t know what to do. I don' t want to or deserve to feel insecure about a girl from his past, I just want to not care about her at all.

Dear Anonymous

I'd say, it's a bit wrong to have past lovers, regardless of the situation, on your social media following them when you're "nothing" it doesn't make much sense to me as well, but sometimes your trust with your partner should have more power than just a follow. If he assures you that you have no problem, believe him, but don't just turn a blind eye to her or the situation. If you keep seeing these happening, then I'd question whether it's something or not. Don't think too much and beat yourself up over something that really could be nothing.

Anyone who's trying to heal,

     The healing process starts when you accept
the pain upfront, whether it was your wrong or
theirs, you need to accept the pain you're left
with is not going to be rekindled into something
attached to love. Every day is another day to move
forward. I can tell you, looking back, I was
searching for answers on how to heal and I was too,
a mess. But it starts with you. You almost never get
closure from the other person because some may never
see wrong in their doings, but that's where you
accept it, and realize there's love out there
waiting to embrace you. Stop searching for answers
to a puzzle that's never going to connect and start
giving yourself the time and love you deserve.
Take care of *YOU*. That's how you heal.

Dear Anonymous

Healing from the unknown can be scary,
because we convince ourselves
closure within the other person is essential,
but forget if find peace
you can move forward,
that's the only closure you need.

Don' t go back searching
for the "old" you,
you' ll find yourself in a circle
of pain, heartache,
lost with no direction.
Don' t go back searching
for the old you,
they don' t exist anymore
It' s time to accept you grew.

Dear Anonymous

A message to a best friend, who became a memory

I'm sorry it came down to which was more important, trying to make you love me, or saving my entire being from becoming lost. I'm sorry for leaving you when I promised I never would. I'm sorry I broke so many promises. I'm sorry my growth scared you, and your eyes saw it as change. I'm sorry you couldn't understand the difference, but always wanted different. I'm sorry you didn't love yourself the way you wanted, so you chose to use my heart for your burdens. I'm sorry you saw me as someone who could be without you, so you chose to push me in that direction. I'm sorry you couldn't find who you were, so you created who you wanted to be, and in the end you never felt whole. I'm sorry I couldn't love you the way you hoped I would. I'm sorry you demanded so much, but never thought what I gave was enough. I'm sorry I couldn't be the friend you wanted me to be. I'm sorry I need to love you from afar. I'm sorry the love we once shared became toxic to us. I'm sorry my soul won't ever get to rest without you. I'm sorry I always seen the soulmate in you. I'm sorry I loved you even when you didn't deserve it. I'm sorry I still do. Healing from someone you'll always love, it's crazy, after all this time there's always love in my heart for you. But when I noticed your absence brought me peace, I knew one thing for sure, I wasn't sorry for choosing me.

Dear Anonymous

Dear Anonymous

Dear Anonymous

Made in the USA
Las Vegas, NV
09 June 2021

24485395R00142